THE 100+ SERIES™

Reproducible Activities

After School
Writing Activities

Grade 5

Published by Instructional Fair • TS Denison
an imprint of

McGraw Hill **Children's Publishing**

Editors: Susan Fitzgerald, Bruce Walker

 Children's Publishing

Published by Instructional Fair • TS Denison
An imprint of McGraw-Hill Children's Publishing
Copyright © 2003 McGraw-Hill Children's Publishing

All Rights Reserved • Printed in the United States of America

Send all inquiries to:
McGraw-Hill Children's Publishing
3195 Wilson Drive NW
Grand Rapids, Michigan 49544

After School Writing Activities—grade 5
ISBN: 0-7424-1785-9

1 2 3 4 5 6 7 8 9 PHXBK 08 07 06 05 04 03
The *McGraw-Hill* Companies

Table of Contents

Introduction

The activities in this book are designed for students to enjoy as after school activities to enhance their writing techniques and skills. These exercises will help students appreciate the beauty and sound of words, feel and hear the rhythms found in sentences, and learn the poetry and subtleties of language. Although these exercises are in simple-to-follow formats, each was created to be fun while communicating a fundamental writing skill.

In these activities, students will read, research, tell stories, design, dramatize, select, evaluate, collect, and share. They will perform narrative, descriptive, expository, and persuasive writing for both fiction and nonfiction. They will have many opportunities to experiment with language, using a variety of writing forms such as journals, book reports, fables, poetry, personal narratives, newspaper stories, puzzles, plays, cloze activities, and story starters.

A cloze activity is a fun writing tool, which encourages creativity and story building skills for the young writer. Students choose their own verbs, adjectives, adverbs, and nouns to fill in the line and complete each story. This is a wonderful way for them to use their imagination as well as practice their grammar skills.

A story starter is also a fun writing tool that starts students on their way to creating their own story by giving them the first sentence of a story.

Every activity is reproducible to share with friends or cut out of the book to work on independently. They could also be used as pages for homework. Some exercises can be completed in one writing period but others may take longer.

Each student should have a notebook to use as a journal, folders or three-ring binders for completed writing projects, and a separate book for poetry. Students will enjoy reading through their compositions. With a separate book of poetry, they can also illustrate their poems.

0-7424-1785-9 *After School Writing Activities*

descriptive verbs   Name _____ Date _____

Fun with Descriptive Verbs

A good writer chooses verbs to express an idea in the most descriptive way. Use the most **exact** and **interesting** verb to show the action in a sentence.

1. Think of one or more verbs that could be used instead of *walked* in the following sentence that show the ideas below. The first one has been done to get you started.

The girl <u>walked</u> to the park.

    a. happy   *skipped*   *pranced* _____

    b. quickly _____

    c. clumsy _____

    d. painful _____

2. Write more interesting verbs for the verb *said* in the following sentence to show the ideas below.

The boy <u>said</u>, "I did it."

    a. excited _____

    b. sad _____

    c. loud _____

    d. confused _____

Look through a newspaper with a friend. Circle or highlight verbs that show actions in the stories.

Name _____ Date _____

Nature's Grand Light Show

Specific words tell the reader more than vague or unclear words.

vague sentence: The lights showed in the sky.

vivid verb: The lights **danced** in the sky.

vague sentence: The lights floated above the planet.

specific names: The **northern lights** floated above the earth.

vague sentence: He saw colors in the sky.

specific words: He saw **violet**, **red**, and **blue** lights in the **midnight** sky.

Circle the letter of the sentences below that are the most specific in describing the topic.

1. Topic: the beams of the northern lights

    a. The beams of the northern lights shine in the night sky of North America.

    b. The fantastic beams of the northern lights shine beautifully.

    c. The beams of the northern lights shimmer with violet, blue, and red colors.

2. Topic: lights are seen in lands in the north

    a. The lights can be seen in North America, northern Europe, and Siberia.

    b. The fantastic lights of the northern lights glowed beautifully in the northern skies.

    c. Violets, reds, and blues dance mysteriously in the northern lights.

3. Topic: how the northern lights look

    a. The lights of the northern lights glow in the sky.

    b. The lights of the northern lights look like beams of colors fanning across the sky.

    c. The lights of the northern lights captivate every person who sees them.

Write a paragraph using specific words to persuade a friend to go see the northern lights. Have a friend do the same and discuss the specific words you both used.

Name _____ Date _____

Picture It!

A good writer uses words to paint a picture for the reader. Interesting writing allows the reader to see something in his or her mind. When writing, **don't tell** the reader what he or she should see; **show** the reader.

tell: The grasslands were beautiful.

show: The prairie grasslands glistened with the early morning dew. Buttery, yellow wildflowers bloomed in the grass. The cool air of dawn smelled sweet.

Write **show** or **tell** in front of each sentence to explain how the writer used the words.

_____ **1.** There was a storm. The sea was rough. The water was blue and white.

_____ **2.** The storm churned the deep blue ocean, throwing the waves high into the air. The waves foamed white as they turned back to the scraggy shore.

In each oval, draw what you see when you read the sentence underneath the oval.

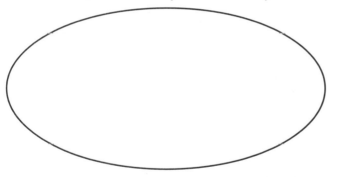 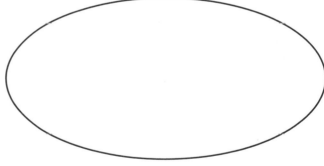

3. It was a nice day.   **4.** The sun beamed brilliantly on the grassy meadow where children flew colorful kites.

5. Which sentence paints a better picture?_____ Why?_____

_____

Choose a favorite place you like to go to with friends. Have a friend choose one too. Write sentences **showing, not telling,** why you like these places. Use plenty of details. Trade descriptions and talk about what place you each chose, and how you described it.

© McGraw-Hill Children's Publishing   0-7424-1785-9 *After School Writing Activities*

Name _____ Date _____

Crooked Castle

The story below is missing descriptive words. Write an adjective or adverb on each line that would make the story more intriguing.

Remember, *adjectives* tell more about a noun and *adverbs* tell more about a verb.

Atop a(n) _____ _____ island stood a(n) _____

_____ castle. It was covered in _____ moss from the

outside walls to the _____ tower. Dylan stood _____ at the foot of the hill leading

to the castle and took a _____ _____ breath. He _____ began to

climb. When he reached the top, he noticed the _____ _____ door

was open. He _____ peaked inside. The room was _____ and smelled

_____. It was too _____ to see. If only he had a flashlight

and a little more courage, Dylan would see the _____

_____ diamonds.

Write an ending to the story. Have a friend write one too. Remember to use descriptive words! Compare your endings and the words you used to describe them.

The Street Is Alive

Personification means giving human qualities to animals or objects. Underline all of the examples of personification in the paragraphs below.

Example: The leaves <u>skipped</u> and <u>danced</u> down the city sidewalks.

1. Every autumn, the farmers' market bustles with activity. The city streets give way to pedestrians swarming the farmers' stalls. An abundance of fruit and vegetables from the fall harvest crowd the tiny stalls. Now that the wind breathes a chill into the air, everything must be picked from the fields and orchards. The stalls are dressed with corn stalks, scarecrows, and pumpkins. Scents from the apple cider, hot dog, and peanut vendors beckon the shoppers. The street is alive with throngs of people enjoying the sights and sounds of market day.

2. The autumn chill threatens to release the warmth in the air and soil, which sustained us through the summer months. Trees wear their brightest colors. It's as if the leaves are attending a ball as they swing, swirl, and waltz slowly toward the ground. When the last of the leaves are still able to dance, winter blows in and sings a different song.

Write your own descriptions to personify each object or animal. Remember, to personify means to give them human qualities.

3. moon
4. parakeet
5. car
6. summer
7. haunted house
8. bear

 Write a paragraph about a thunderstorm using personification. Have a friend do the same and combine your paragraphs to create a story.

Name _____ Date _____

Like a Bowl Full of Jelly

A **simile** compares two things using the words *like* or *as*. These words clearly show that a comparison is being made.

> **Examples:** Grandpa has a mind like a steel trap.
> Emmett's word was as good as gold.

1. Underline five similes in these lines from
"A Visit from Saint Nicholas."
His eyes, how they twinkled! His dimples, how merry!
His cheeks were like roses, his nose like a cherry!
And the beard on his chin was as white as the snow;
The stump of a pipe he held tight in his teeth,
And the smoke it encircled his head like a wreath;
He had a broad face and a round little belly,
That shook when he laughed like a bowl full of jelly.

—*Clement Moore*

2. Complete the following similes. Try to think of colorful comparisons.

　　a. She was as clumsy as _____.

　　b. Billy was as nervous as _____.

　　c. My next-door neighbor has a laugh like _____.

　　d. Yesterday it was as hot as _____.

Write a paragraph describing one of the following situations using similes. Ask a friend to write one too and find the similes in each other's paragraphs.

the cafeteria during lunchtime　　a blizzard
waking up from a nightmare　　the last day of summer vacation

0-7424-1785-9 *After School Writing Activities*

Name _____ Date _____

As Gentle as a Lamb

Using **similes** in writing to compare things can make your meaning more clear.

Examples: Uncle Emilio has a voice like a cannon.

My little sister is as gentle as a lamb.

Angela was as white as a ghost.

Write a word from the Word Bank on the lines below
to complete these similes.

Word Bank
rock swan
drums fish

1. Her long, lovely neck made her seem as graceful as a _____.

2. The thunder boomed like distant _____.

3. Mallory won the swim meet because she swims like a _____.

4. The coach's promise is as solid as a _____.

Complete the similes below to describe the turtle, boat, mayor, and Max.

5. Dad remembers that giant turtle from when he was a boy.

   That turtle is as big as _____.

6. I carried the boat over the rocks. It wasn't too heavy.

   The boat is as light as _____.

7. When the mayor spoke, everyone could hear him.

   The mayor is as loud as _____.

8. After coming in from playing in the snow, Max's nose was frozen.

   His nose was as cold as _____.

Write six similes with a friend to describe your favorite animal.

Name _____ Date _____

You're a Dream Come True

A **metaphor** compares two things <u>without</u> using *like* or *as*. You can use a word or phrase, which means one thing to describe another to make your writing more colorful and imaginative.

Examples: You're a dream come true. You are wonderful.

That mountain is a monster. No one has ever been able to climb it.

Read the sentences below. Circle the letter of the sentences that tell what the metaphor means.

1. My brother is a workhorse.
   a. My brother is big.
   b. My brother smells like hay.
   c. My brother works hard.

2. George was a tiger on the prowl.
   a. George was growling with anger.
   b. George was wearing my striped pajamas.
   c. George was very quiet and sneaky.

3. Mr. McKnight is a dinosaur.
   a. Mr. McKnight has rough skin.
   b. Mr. McKnight likes dinosaurs.
   c. Mr. McKnight is out of touch with new ideas.

4. That final exam was a bear.
   a. The final exam was about types of bears.
   b. The final exam was very hard.
   c. My stomach was growling during the final exam.

Write your own metaphors with a friend for two of the items below. Combine your sentences to create a paragraph about the subject.

a man who works very slowly   a spring day
a stingy person   an old, worn-out car

Name _____ Date _____

As Sweet as Pie

A **simile** compares two things using the word *like* or *as*.
Example: He was as stubborn as a mule.

A **metaphor** compares two things <u>without</u> using the word *like* or *as*.
Example: He is a mule.

Write an **S** for simile or an **M** for metaphor to tell what type of comparison is made in each sentence. Then, write down what the simile or metaphor might mean.

____ **1.** Mr. Habeeb is a packrat.

_____

_____

____ **2.** Josephine is as sweet as pie.

_____

_____

____ **3.** Maury sometimes rages like a storm.

_____

_____

_____

_____

____ **4.** That guy is a weasel.

_____

_____

____ **5.** The thief was as slippery as an eel.

_____

_____

____ **6.** The sunset is a painter's palette

_____

_____

____ **7.** I slept like a baby.

_____

_____

____ **8.** Mary is a bookworm.

_____

_____

I Could Sleep for a Year!

A **hyperbole** is an extreme exaggeration. Use a hyperbole to emphasize your point.
Example: I'm so tired that I could sleep for a year!

Write an **H** if the sentence is a hyperbole. Otherwise, leave the line blank.

_____ **1.** I am so hungry that I could eat a horse!

_____ **2.** That box weighs a ton.

_____ **3.** Hercules was very strong.

_____ **4.** That hole is so deep it goes
straight through to China.

_____ **5.** Ramon can run faster
than anyone I know.

_____ **6.** I jumped so high that I hit
my head on the moon

_____ **7.** We scared Mrs. Bradshaw to death.

Write your own hyperboles, or exaggerations, for these sentences.
Remember to write in complete sentences.

8. I was thirsty. _____

_____

9. George's bedroom was clean. _____

_____

10. Michelle's sandwich was big. _____

_____

11. I was late. _____

_____

Read a tall tale with a friend. How many hyperboles did you find
in your story? Write your own tall tales. Remember to use hyperboles.

Name _____ Date _____

Whirl!

Onomatopoeia (ON-uh-MOT-uh-PEE-ya) is the use of words that imitate natural sounds. Using these words makes writing more interesting.

Examples: All you could hear at night in the campground was the **crackle** of fire from the campfires.

My brother made a big **splash** when he jumped into the pool.

Read these sentences. Write the words that are examples of onomatopoeia on the lines.

1. The tornado whirled over the lake. _____

2. The woods were so quiet, we could hear a twig snap. _____

3. The windows rattled as the hurricane got closer to shore. _____

Underline any words in this selection that sound like their meanings.

4. The marsh behind Kitty's house is filled with sound. Toads and tree frogs ribbit at nightfall. Sometimes the chirping of the crickets drowns out the sounds of the little frogs. But the croak of the big bullfrogs can always be heard. Each bird has a unique song, too. There are blaring caws, gentle whistles, and cheery trills. Even the buzz of mosquitoes can be heard in the marsh. I don't know how Kitty sleeps with all that racket going on!

Ribbit

Visit the zoo or a farm with a friend. Write paragraphs about your trip using at least six words that show onomatopoeia.

Name _____ Date _____

Answer, Respond, Reply Crossword

Synonyms are words that have the same or nearly the same meaning.

Fill in the blanks with synonyms of the verbs listed below. To help you along, some of the letters have been given.

Across

1. desire
4. trample
7. tilt
9. loan
12. spoke
14. lift
15. fasten
16. awaken
19. mimics
20. placed
21. matured
24. sparkled
27. hurry
28. throw
30. fibs
32. carries
36. capture
37. explode
38. mistake
39. haul
40. decay
41. love
42. frighten
43. caught
44. scan
45. operate

Down

1. strolls
2. liquid for writing
3. rob
5. labored
6. encounter
7. halt
8. intertwined
10. escape
11. fantasize
13. tow
15. disembark
17. lubricate
18. foam
22. obtain
23. break
25. dined
26. tap
27. sleeps
28. phone
29. frightens
30. bait
31. presses
32. rip
33. arrange
34. trampled
35. talk
36. allege

0-7424-1785-9 *After School Writing Activities*

Name _____ Date _____

Lost and Found Crossword

Antonyms are words that have opposite meanings.

Fill in the blanks with antonyms of the words listed below. To help you along, some of the letters have been given.

Across

2. more
5. dry
8. fast
11. below
13. off
16. morning
17. cries
20. yes
21. borrowed
22. know
23. bad
24. go
25. him
26. she

27. few
28. daughter
31. women
33. in
35. wrong
39. disobey
41. disown
43. talker
44. sink
45. live
46. fierce
47. dry
48. crooked

Down

1. pa
2. hated
3. odd
4. received
5. weak
6. well
7. tender
9. lad
10. lost
12. above
14. all
15. smaller
18. host
19. villain

24. accept
26. cold
29. later
30. us
31. your
32. old
34. over
36. busy
37. stay
38. fat
39. young
40. west
42. came
44. land

0-7424-1785-9 *After School Writing Activities*

Name _____ Date _____

Good Grief!

An **oxymoron** is a combination of two words that have opposite meanings.

Example: Tony was <u>clearly</u> <u>confused</u> by the instructions.

Underline the oxymoron in the sentences below.

1. There was a calm wind off the lake.

2. My favorite character in the Wizard of Oz
is the cowardly lion.

3. When Lucretia told me about the new kid on the block, I told her it was old news.

4. The iguana we saw at the zoo was pretty ugly.

Write a sentence using each oxymoron below.

act naturally	small crowd
good grief	terribly pleased
second best	seriously funny

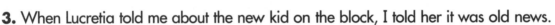

_____

_____

_____

_____

_____

Work with a friend to think of an oxymoron to describe your bedroom,
your classroom, a brother or sister, and a pet.

0-7424-1785-9 *After School Writing Activities*

Combining Words

Combine a word from List A with a word from List B to form a new word that fits the definition. The first one is done for you.

List A				
ad	be	bed	car	eye
hand	hum	lady	mush	news
pal	per	pig	port	rebel

List B				
able	ace	age	brow	bug
form	lion	long	or	paper
room	shake	tail	time	ton

List A	+	List B	=	New Word	Definition
news	+	paper	=	newspaper	1. daily paper contains news
_____	+	_____	=	_____	2. curve of hair above eye
_____	+	_____	=	_____	3. not fixed or stationary
_____	+	_____	=	_____	4. to be part of
_____	+	_____	=	_____	5. royalty's home
_____	+	_____	=	_____	6. wit
_____	+	_____	=	_____	7. cardboard box
_____	+	_____	=	_____	8. where you go to sleep
_____	+	_____	=	_____	9. round red insect with black spots
_____	+	_____	=	_____	10. tight braid of hair
_____	+	_____	=	_____	11. an uprising
_____	+	_____	=	_____	12. two people clasping hands
_____	+	_____	=	_____	13. a wise saying
_____	+	_____	=	_____	14. an edible fungus
_____	+	_____	=	_____	15. to act

0-7424-1785-9 *After School Writing Activities*

Name _____ Date _____

Fun with Word Endings

Use the **word endings** in the box below to change the words into the parts of speech indicated after the word (noun, adverb, adjective). Then write a sentence using the new word.

Word Endings						
-ic	-al	-dom	-fy	-ness	-or	-en
-y	-ed	-ly	-ace	-ism	-er	-ure
-ous	-ize	-ice	-ity	-ence	-ar	-less
-tion	-ment	-ish	-ty	-ance	-ship	

1. To act (noun) _____

_____

2. Polite (adverb) _____

_____

3. Trick (adjective) _____

_____

4. Free (noun) _____

_____

Use four word endings from the box above to create new words from the word *friend.* Write your new words on line 5.

5. _____, _____, _____, _____

Ask a friend to help you think of words you can make from the words below by adding word endings from the box above. Write sentences using your new words.

nice   charm   fair   like

Name _____ Date _____

Combining Sentences

Make as many sentences as possible with the information from the first group of sentences. Each sentence must be correct and make sense. You may only use information that appears in the sentences.

Example: Margo is sitting in her car smiling when she calls out to her friend.

Margo calls out to her friend. Margo is smiling. Margo has her purse. Margo is sitting in her car. It is Saturday. It is a sunny day. The friend gets into her car. Margo wants to go shopping.

_____

_____

_____

_____

_____

_____

 Using the group of sentences below, make as many sentences as possible and have a friend do the same. See who can make the most correct sentences.

The animals are wild. The animals live in the jungle. The animals hunt for food in packs. The animals kill the tribe's chickens. The tribe wants to trap the animals. The tribe hunts the animals.

_____

_____

_____

_____

_____

 0-7424-1785-9 *After School Writing Activities*

Name _____ Date _____

Getting to the New World

The order or **sequence** of sentences is very important in some paragraphs. Using **transition words** help to show the sequence of the sentences.

Before Christopher Columbus could leave to discover the New World, there were many things he had to do. The events below are numbered in the correct order. Choose transition words from the box below to write these events into a complete paragraph. The topic sentence is written for you.

1. He studied maps and thought he could sail west to Asia.

2. He asked the king of Portugal for ships, but the king refused to help Columbus.

3. He asked for a royal commission from Spain for ships, but they would not help him.

4. In 1492, King Ferdinand and Queen Isabella, rulers of two Spanish kingdoms, gave him the ships he needed for the voyage.

5. Columbus set sail for Asia, but he discovered the Americas instead.

<u>Christopher Columbus had many things to do before he could begin his journey.</u>

Transition Words	
Finally,	_____
Another,	_____
First,	_____
Often,	_____
Second,	_____
One,	_____
Next,	_____
Then,	_____
Once,	_____

Name _____ Date _____

Jolly Gerbil Jamboree

Consonance is a consonant sound repeated anywhere in a series of words.

    Example: The **j**olly **g**erbil went to the **j**amboree with his girlfriend **J**eanine.

Alliteration is a beginning consonant sound repeated in a series of words.

    Example: **F**ireman **F**redo **f**ought the **f**ire on the corner of **F**ranklin and **F**remont.

Assonance is a vowel sound repeated anywhere in a series of words. Remember that vowels and combinations of vowels can make more than one sound.

    Example: Suz**e**tte hoped that her p**e**t would g**e**t b**e**tter.

Read each sentence. Write on each line whether it's an example of consonance, alliteration, or assonance. Also, underline the letter sound or sounds that are repeated.

1. _____ Six swans swam by.

2. _____ The doctor delivered a baby boy.

3. _____ They were glad that we got to ride in a sleigh today.

4. _____ Mr. Reilly really wanted to ride on a roller coaster.

5. _____ Helene sighed when I replied that we couldn't look for shells because of the rising tide.

6. _____ Two taxi drivers tackled the thief.

Write your own sentences using consonance, alliteration, and assonance. Have a friend do the same, then exchange sentences and write a paragraph based on each sentence.

Name _____ Date _____

All the King's Horses

Quotation marks show a character's exact words. Put quotation marks outside of the punctuation that is included in the quote. Capitalize the first word of the quote, unless the quote is a partial sentence. Separate a quotation from the rest of the sentence with a comma, question mark, or exclamation point.

Examples: "Nature wears one universal grin," stated Henry Fielding.

"All the King's horses and all the King's men," the child recited, "couldn't put Humpty together again."

Ella Wheeler Wilcox wrote, "Laugh, and the world laughs with you."

"Nature is your fortune. Treasure it above all."

Add the correct punctuation to these quotations.

1. Benjamin Franklin said Early to bed and early to rise makes a man healthy wealthy and wise

2. Today whatever may annoy the word for me is Joy just simple Joy said John Kendrick Bangs

3. I am always doing that which I can not do Pablo Picasso stated in order that I may learn to do it

4. Robert Fripp said Music is the wine that fills the cup of silence

5. A boy can learn a lot from a dog: obedience, loyalty, and the importance of turning around three times before lying down said Robert Benchley.

Go with a friend to the library and take out books that include conversation. Notice the quotation marks while you're reading. Copy a conversation from the book without using any quotation marks or punctuation. Have your friend do the same and switch papers to correctly place the marks.

Name _____ Date _____

Writing Conversation

A **dialogue** is a conversation between two or more people. Reading what a character says reveals much about the character and the situation.

Read this dialogue between Mrs. Gable, Maxine's mother, and Ms. Gomez, Maxine's teacher.

"Maxine's always been a good girl," Mrs. Gable said quietly.

Ms. Gomez scowled before she spoke. "I've been annoyed by Maxine's behavior this week. She brought ten white mice to my classroom on Tuesday. It made math class impossible."

"Well, scientists often use white mice—"

"Not during math tests, Mrs. Gable." The teacher's dark eyes blazed. "Replacing the cook's sugar with salt in the lunchroom, however, was the last straw!"

Think about what you've learned about the characters. Then, continue the conversation on the lines below.

_____

_____

_____

_____

_____

Write dialogue for the situation below or make up your own situation. Discuss the situation with a friend and carry on a conversation as you imagine your characters would. Then, write the conversation down.

A discussion between two squirrels about which park is the best in town.

Name _____ Date _____

My First Day

Narrative writing tells a story. Use a **story map** to plan a story.

Plan a story by making a story map from these ideas. Write the ideas into the plan where they fit best.

- First, Mr. Brunswick introduced me to the other kids in the class.
- beginning of fifth grade
- Then, one plucky boy said he'd show me around the school.
- Mr. Brunswick, the class, and me
- Finally, other kids welcomed me to Seattle and Hillcrest Elementary School.
- Hillcrest Elementary School
- My family moved to Seattle this summer. I'm the new kid here.
- Next, some of the kids teased me about my southern accent.

Story Map

1. **a.** setting: _____
   b. characters: _____
   c. problem: _____

2. first event: _____
   _____

3. second event: _____
   _____

4. third event: _____
   _____

5. resolution: _____
   _____

Write a story about the new student using the story map above. Have a friend write a story using the same story map. Read each other's stories and see how they're different.

Name _____ Date _____

Bigfoot

Outlining is a good way to keep your information and paragraphs in order or sequence when you are writing. If you outline, you can plot the sequence before you write. This makes writing a story much easier.

Below is some information about the Bigfoot or Sasquatch mystery.
List each fact under the proper heading in the outline that follows.

- Bigfoot lives in wilderness areas of North America, especially the Pacific northwest.
- Bigfoot has brownish fur, is half-man, half-ape, and is up to or over seven feet tall
- In 1967, a Bigfoot was caught on film by Roger Patterson in northwest California.
- The man-like creature may simply be a large bear.
- Human-shaped tracks were discovered from 12 inches to 17 inches long.
- When bear tracks in snow melt, they may look like huge footprints.
- Bigfoot is sometimes seen near remote villages or towns.
- Cultural histories of Native Americans include many stories and beliefs of a hairy, man-like creature.
- There have been several expeditions and sightings.
- Bigfoot walks erect on thick legs.

I. What is it?

  A. Appearance

    1. _____

    2. _____

  B. Where is it found?

    1. _____

    2. _____

II. Does it really exist?

  A. Evidence

    1. _____

    2. _____

    3. _____

    4. _____

  B. Explanations

    1. _____

    2. _____

Get together with a friend and pretend you have found the huge tracks of a Bigfoot in the woods. Based on the outline above and your imagination, write a story together about your experience.

Name _____ Date _____

Writing Instructions

In order to do anything—make a sandwich or give your dog a bath—you have to carry out a number of steps in the right order, or **sequence**. Words like *first*, *next*, *then*, and *finally* help show the sequence.

Here is a list of steps for making a papier-mâché pumpkin. They are not in the correct sequence. Write them in the correct order on the lines below.

1. When the newspaper is dry, cut a hole in the bottom, burst the ballon, and paint it orange.

2. Cut up 2 inch strips of newspaper and dip into the mixture.

3. Cut out a face for the pumpkin.

4. Apply the strips to the balloon.

5. Blow up a round balloon and tie the end.

6. Mix two parts water with one part flour.

7. Stir until the mixture is smooth, sticky, and wet.

First: _____

Next: _____

Then: _____

Fourth: _____

Fifth: _____

Sixth: _____

Finally: _____

Write instructions with a friend for doing the following—making an ice-cream sundae, making a paper airplane, or doing a cartwheel.

Name _____ Date _____

Walfredo and the Cat

The **plot** is the plan, or series of events, in a story. The **events** in the story are often attempts made to solve the main character's problem. Often there are added troubles for the main character. The events build to a **climax**, which is the point of the most forceful action in the story. It comes right before the end of the story, which is called the **resolution**.

Read the problem. Then, circle the paragraphs that might be part of the story's action.

1. Problem: Walfredo is supposed to play the saxophone at the Mouse King's Ball, but he has to get past the cat first.

a. Walfredo built a paper airplane to fly off the kitchen counter and over the cat. He was too heavy and the plane crashed. Walfredo had to run for cover!

b. The next day, the Mouse King sent soldiers to arrest Walfredo.

c. A dog began to bark when a car drove past the house.

d. Walfredo practiced the saxophone for many years.

e. The King once gave Walfredo a new saxophone.

f. Walfredo hummed lullabies, trying to get the cat to fall asleep. The cat yawned but never fell asleep.

g. Walfredo shot some rubber bands at the cat, but the cat did not move.

h. The cat had made many attempts to catch the clever mouse, but the cat had only come close to catching him once.

i. Walfredo flicked the kitchen lights to send a message to the Mouse King. The king sent soldiers to distract the cat.

2. Choose the best climax for this story. Remember, the climax has the most forceful action.

a. Walfredo gets caught by the cat, but the Mouse King's troops rescue him.

b. Walfredo waits so long for the cat to fall asleep that he misses the ball.

c. Walfredo runs past the cat but is too late to play the saxophone at the ball.

Write your own climax idea for this story and have a friend write the resolution.

Name _____ Date _____

Developing Characters

Before creating fictional characters, it helps to **observe** real people. Being a good observer helps you to become a good writer. The little things about someone or something are often the details that bring the story to life for the reader.

Observation is a two-step process. First, the writer takes notes on what he or she is observing. Later, those notes are used to create paragraphs. Below are notes taken during the observation of someone in a park. With Step 1 completed for you, go on to Step 2 and write a paragraph about this person based on the notes.

Step 1: Notes

man in the park—lean, muscular—age is early 20s—medium height—white T-shirt —blue-jean shorts—watch on left wrist—buzz cut, brown hair—red, high top tennis shoes— carrying a bouquet of flowers—running slowly—drizzly day—doesn't seem to notice rain

Step 2: Paragraph _____

_____

_____

_____

_____

With a friend, choose someone to observe. Take separate notes, then use your notes to write a paragraph. Exchange your paragraphs. Note the differences in your observations and how you used them to write your paragraphs. Work together to combine your paragraphs and expand them into a story.

Name _____ Date _____

Describing Characters

Describing a character's appearance, qualitites, and actions paints a picture for the reader.

Read this description of Ichabod Crane from *The Legend of Sleepy Hollow*. These details paint a picture for you of what Ichabod Crane looked like.

> He was tall but exceedingly lank, with narrow shoulders, long arms and legs, hands that dangled a mile out of his sleeves, feet that might have served for shovels, and his whole frame hung together most loosely. His head was small and flat at top, with huge ears, large green glassy eyes, and a long snipe nose, so that it looked like a weathercock perched upon his spindle neck...
>
> —*Washington Irving*

Describe a real or fictional person's appearance and qualities. Character qualities show what a person is like, such as brave, nervous, intelligent, proud, nice, or mean. Use the following list to record important details.

Face: _____

Hair: _____

Size: _____

Clothes: _____

Gestures and Movements: _____

Qualities:_____

Using the details you wrote down for the character above, work with a friend to describe this character in one of the following situations. Be funny or true to life.

the power has gone out during
a thunderstorm
a block party on your street

someone's first visit to a farm or big city
a train or subway ride

A Day in Your Life

You can write about a character using different points of view.

Here are some examples.

Scenario 1 (character talking to self):
What's that awful noise? Is that a tornado siren? No, wait a minute. It's that pesky alarm clock! Can it be time to get up already? It's 6:00 A.M.

What day is this? Friday? Yes. Oh, good. There are parent-teacher conferences today, so I don't have school. I can sleep in. Yes!

Scenario 2 (third person—as though someone was watching and writing):
She woke to the sound of a siren. Sleepily, she pulled the covers back over her head and shrunk under them moaning, "I'm too tired to get up right now."

Suddenly, a hand reached over her and the noise stopped.

"You don't have school today honey," her Mom whispered. "There are parent-teacher conferences so you can sleep in."

Scenario 3 (first person—the author is telling the story):
My day begins with the sharp, terrifying noise of the alarm clock. More like a tornado siren than anything else, but there is no escaping its message. Time to get ready for school. The day has begun.

Write about someone getting ready for school. Try writing it from each point of view above.

Write about a day in your life and ask a friend to write about the same day in his or her life. Choose one of the scenarios above to start your story. Remember to take your reader through each part of your day, helping him or her to *see*, *feel*, *smell*, and *taste* everything you do. Read each other's stories.

Name _____ Date _____

Setting the Scene

When and **where** a story takes place are important decisions for the writer. Will it be a murder mystery at a hotel? Will it be an adventure story at a ranch? Will it take place in an art museum, in a wagon train, or on a spaceship?

The story setting helps to express the mood of the story. In order to paint the scene, a writer needs to experience it. That is why many writers research or travel to places they wish to write about.

Here is an example of describing a setting using the two-step process of observation (notes at the scene) and writing.

Step 1: Notes

late afternoon—hot sun suspended over the mountains—mountains cast in shadows of purple and blue—horses grazing in the foothills, swatting flies with their tails—birds chirping and fluttering about in the nearby trees—far-off bark of a dog—the air is still—heavy, sweet scent of orange blossoms and jasmine fills the air

Step 2: Paragraph

As she walked toward her horse's stall, Moria drank in the heavy, sweet scent of orange blossoms and jasmine that filled the still late afternoon air. She stopped for a moment to watch the purple and blue shadows on the mountains beyond. The sun, still hot, was suspended above them, as if placed there. She gazed out at the horses grazing in the foothills, lazily swatting at flies with their tails, and listened to the birds chirping and fluttering about in the trees. Far off, she heard the bark of a dog at play. It was a beautiful place, this California.

Write your own story beginning. Remember to show when and where the story takes place so readers will feel like they are there.

Go to a place with a friend that you would like to use as a setting for a story. Spend some time there, paying close attention to what you *hear, see, smell, taste,* and *feel.* Take your own notes and write your setting descriptions later. Exchange your descriptions to see the differences in your settings and what you observed.

The Great Pyramid

The beginning of a paragraph often **leads** the reader into the story by stating an **interesting fact** or asking an **exciting question**.

Read each paragraph below. Choose the best **lead** for each paragraph and write it on the line. It will be the first sentence of the paragraph.

- Did you know that ancient Egypt played a part in the design of the U.S. dollar bill?

- Pyramids are very large buildings in Egypt.

- Pharaohs had large pyramids built for their tombs.

- The United States dollar was very important in ancient Egypt.

- For 4,300 years, the Great Pyramid of Khufu at Giza was the tallest building in the entire world.

1. _____

_____

When it was built, the pyramid was about 480 feet (146 m) high and was 751 feet (229 m) on each side. It had more than two million stones, each weighing more than two tons. The pyramid was the tomb of the great Egyptian pharaoh, King Khufu. The pyramid held his mummy and the treasures that the Egyptians believed he would need on his journey into the afterlife. Though no longer the tallest building, Khufu's tomb, the Great Pyramid of Giza, is still the largest stone building on earth.

2. _____

_____

A good example of this is the Great Seal of the United States, visible on the back of the dollar bill. Can you see the unfinished pyramid? The pyramid is a sign of strength and permanence. The founding fathers of our country believed that the United States would last like the great pyramids of ancient Egypt. However, because the country would always grow and change, the pyramid was left unfinished in the design of the dollar bill.

Look through magazines and newspapers with a friend to find leads in the very beginning of articles. Did they make you want to read the article?

Name _____ Date _____

Tornado Warning!

A **topic sentence** expresses the main idea in a paragraph. A **lead** interests the reader to read more about the topic. **Supporting sentences** explain more about the main idea. A paragraph often includes at least three key supporting sentences.

Read each topic sentence below and circle three sentences that support each topic.

1. Tornadoes form as a destructive whirling wind with a funnel-shaped cloud when warm air and cold air meet.

   a. They form when the two air masses come together.

   b. States in the Great Plains often have storms.

   c. Warm air rises from the ground, and the storm winds begin to swirl in the sky.

   d. A tornado is extremely dangerous.

   e. When the swirling wind reaches down to the ground, it is called a tornado.

2. Tornado Alley is made up of states in the center of the United States from north to south.

   a. States with mountains do not have many tornadoes.

   b. The states in Tornado Alley have open, flat land, and many storms.

   c. Tornadoes are likely to occur every year in this part of the country.

   d. A tornado warning is issued when a tornado is sighted from the ground or seen on radar.

   e. Texas, Oklahoma, Kansas, and Nebraska are all part of Tornado Alley.

3. A tornado touched down very close to our house last spring.

   a. The sky turned dark, even though it was daytime.

   b. Tornadoes sound like trains.

   c. We could hear the tornado rumble past our windows.

   d. My aunt once saw a tornado while she was driving.

   e. The high winds knocked down our neighbor's tree.

Name _____ Date _____

And She Lived Happily Ever After

The **theme** is the subject or overall message of a story.

Read the short summaries of the stories below. Choose one of the **themes** from the list that best matches each summary. Write the letter of the theme on each line.

Themes
a. Things aren't always what they seem.
b. Honesty is the best policy.
c. Believe in yourself.
d. Good things eventually happen to those who are kind and good.

_____ **1.** Once there was a girl who lived with her stepmother and stepsisters. Although the girl was kind, they were cruel to her. One day, her fairy godmother rewarded her goodness by helping her go to the royal ball. There, she met a prince and fell in love.

_____ **2.** Once Joey took a small apple from a fruit stand. He knew it was wrong, but he didn't have enough money, and he really wanted the apple. The next day, he went back and apologized to Mr. Chin, the owner of the stand. Mr. Chin was a kind man and understood. He gave Joey a job after school so he not only could pay for the apple, but also earn money for his family.

_____ **3.** The mean old man glared at Carrie. All she did was say hello. She tried so many times to be nice to Mr. Moleski, but he didn't seem to care. Her mother told her that Mr. Moleski's wife died many years ago and he was a sad man. Carrie asked if their family could have Mr. Moleski come for dinner. Thanks to Carrie's kindness, Mr. Moleski smiled again.

_____ **4.** The boys asked Alfonso to join their basketball team. The only problem was that Alfonso didn't know how to play. First, he told the others he was sick. The next time they asked him, Alfonso said his family was going somewhere. He was embarrassed that he didn't know how to play. Finally, he couldn't hide it anymore. The others taught Alfonso to play, and it turned out he was a great player. He had worried for no reason at all.

Go to the library with a friend and take out books of fairy tales. After you both read a few stories, discuss the theme of each fairy tale. Using the theme of your favorite fairy tale, write your own short story.

Name _____ Date _____

It's All in a Name

The **title** is a very important part of a story. It should give a hint about the subject of a story, but it should not give away the ending.

Example: *One in a Million*

The first word, the last word, and all of the important words in a title are capitalized. When book titles are printed in books or articles, they are in italics, *like this*. When you write a book title, underline it.

In a book: *My Piece of the Pie*
When you write it: <u>My Piece of the Pie</u>

Pick the best title for this passage of a story. Remember, a good title doesn't give away too much.

1. The summit appeared several feet away. Mario's feet ached from supporting his weight on the tiny ledge. Suddenly, his brother's face emerged just above him. Pedro let down the rope to Mario and pulled him to safety. Together, they triumphed over the wall of granite known as White Mountain.

    a. *Triumph Over White Mountain*   **c.** *Challenging the Mountain*

    b. *Mario and Pedro*   **d.** *Safe Mountain Climbing*

Write a title for the passage of the story below.

2. _____

The rope weakened as the impressive wild horse labored against his tether. When he reared and struck down at the rope with his hooves, the rope broke, releasing him. Untamed and free, this beautiful creature galloped across the rich, brown soil. With his nostrils flaring, he breathed in the smell of freedom.

Write new titles for your favorite books with a friend. Write a title for a book about the history of your city or town. Write new names for yourselves. How did you decide what the titles and names would be?

Name _____ Date _____

The Sum of the Elements

All of the words in the Word Bank are important elements that you use in writing. Complete the crossword using these words.

Word Bank

transitions
plot
hook
point of view
resolution
beginning
middle
end
dialogue
setting
climax
characters
title
conflict

Across

6. the last part of a story

7. shows who is telling the story

10. gets the reader's interest

11. highest point of action

12. events leading to a climax

13. how a story starts

14. people, animals, or things that do
or say something in a story

Down

1. words used to show the order or relationship of events

2. the body of the story

3. the name of the story

4. how the problem is solved

5. the problem or difficulty

8. where and when the story takes place

9. characters talking in a story

Choose a book that both you and a friend would like to read. As you each read it separately, identify all of the story parts. When you've both finished reading it, discuss the conflict. How was it resolved? What was the climax?

foreshadowing   Name _____ Date _____

What's Happening?

Foreshadowing is hinting or offering clues to the reader about what will happen in the story.

> **Example:** Nothing unusual ever happens at the school spelling bee, or so we thought.
> (This hints that something unexpected will happen.)

Each paragraph below hints about something that might happen. Underline the words or sentences below that make you think this and then write what you think might happen.

1. Dirk boasted to everyone at the basketball game as his brother stepped up to the free throw line. "My brother gets a basket whenever he shoots," Dirk cried out. Boy, was he dumbfounded.

_____

_____

_____

2. Everyone was already on the bus for the field trip to the art museum. Emmie looked pale and the teacher asked her if she felt sick. Emmie told her she felt fine. Actually, she felt a little sick to her stomach, but at the time, she thought it was nothing to worry about.

_____

_____

_____

3. Billy was the smartest boy in the school. He always got the highest grade on every test. No one expected what happened after the last History test.

_____

_____

_____

Write a story beginning with a hint about what might happen. See if your friends can guess what is going to happen next in your story.

Name _____ Date _____

Mrs. O'Leary's Cow

A **paragraph** is a group of sentences that tell the reader about one main idea.
If sentences do not support the main idea, they do not belong in the paragraph.

Read each paragraph below and circle the letter of the sentence following the paragraph that tells
the main idea. Cross out one sentence in each paragraph that does not support the main idea.

1. Most people know that Chicago is called the Windy City. People have many
ideas about how Chicago got this nickname. Some say that it's because a group of people
bragged about the city constantly to try to get Chicago chosen as the site for the 1893 World's
Fair. People in cities chose school boards, too. A newspaper editor wrote that people shouldn't
believe all the claims of "that windy city". Now you know one possible reason why Chicago is
called the Windy City.

    a. Chicago is called the Windy City because people bragged about it so much.

    b. Editors who write about windy cities run their newspapers like businesses.

2. Chicago is well known for the great fire that swept through the city in 1871.
It burned for three days and destroyed about one-third of the city. The homes of more than
90,000 people burned down and more than 250 people lost their lives. Fires cause a lot of
damage all around the world. No one knows exactly how the fire started. Some people think
Mrs. O'Leary's cow kicked over a lantern. Then the lantern started a fire behind someone's
house. Because of a long dry spell, the fire spread quickly and grew into the fire that became
part of Chicago's history.

    a. A cow started the great fire of 1871.

    b. The great fire of 1871 destroyed part of Chicago.

With a friend, look up a story about an event in the history of your city or town.
Using the same lead sentence, write supporting sentences
to describe this event and combine them to create a story.

Name _____ Date _____

Wrapping It Up

A paragraph may have a **concluding sentence** at the end of the paragraph. It reminds the reader of the main idea and wraps up the supporting sentences, giving the reader something to think about or asking a question.

Circle the letter of the best concluding sentence for these paragraphs.

1. Of all the rooms in my house, I spend the most time in the kitchen. It's the center of activity for everything that happens in our family. For example, it's where Dad told us we were going to Disneyland. Mom puts our drawings and paintings on the refrigerator so it's like a family art show in our kitchen! Another reason I spend so much time in the kitchen is because my Mom is such a great cook. The smell of bacon, cookies, or home-baked bread often fills the air.

    a. My bedroom is another wonderful room in our house.

    b. I wonder if everyone enjoys spending time in their kitchen as much as my family does?

    c. My house is a wonderful place to live.

2. Other people have pets they love, but my dog, Sasha, is the sweetest dog on earth. She never barks at me. She only barks at strangers, which makes her a good watchdog. Another reason Sasha is great is because she is nice to other dogs. She never growls, and she stays by my side during our walks. Finally, Sasha always comes when I call her. She runs like the wind to get to me, and then sits so I can pat her on the head.

    a. I feel so lucky to have such a good dog for a pet.

    b. Sasha is very smart, and she learns tricks easily.

    c. I think dogs make the best possible pets.

Write a paragraph about what goes on in your kitchen. Ask a friend to write one about his or her kitchen. Don't write a concluding sentence for your paragraphs. Describe what you hear, see, smell, taste, and feel. Trade paragraphs and write the concluding sentence for each other's paragraph.

Name _____ Date _____

The Broadway Musical

A **descriptive paragraph** gives information or explains something by painting a picture in the reader's mind. Using all five senses—*sight, sound, smell, taste,* and *touch*—to describe something makes a paragraph more interesting.

Write down the sense—sight, sound, smell, taste, or touch —that best describes each thing. Then write words or phrases to show how that sense describes it. The first one is done for you.

thing	sense	description
1. chocolate caramels	taste, smell	sweet, chewy, sugary, delicious
2. orchestra		
3. audience		
4. spotlight		
5. theater seats		
6. costumes		
7. perfume		
8. dancer		

with a friend

Write descriptions of things you've seen or experienced at a theater. Ask a friend to write about his or her own experience. Remember to "paint a picture" for your reader by using different senses. Compare each other's stories.

42
0-7424-1785-9 *After School Writing Activities*

Where—Mystery at the Museum

Make a sentence more interesting by **adding details** and **explanations** to tell *how, when,* or *where* something happens.

Detective Walker is asking the people in the museum questions. Help him by circling the sentences that give the most details and explanations he needs to solve the case.
(Hint: the correct sentences the detective needs must tell *how, when,* and *where.*)

Basic sentence:　　Detective Walker searched the museum.

Adding how:　　Detective Walker searched the museum carefully.

Adding when:　　Detective Walker searched the museum carefully for two days.

Adding where:　　Detective Walker searched every room and office of the museum carefully for two days.

1. Where was Mr. Maxon when the keys disappeared?

   a. Mr. Maxon was cleaning a glass case with a cloth.

   b. Mr. Maxon was in the Rock Room wiping a glass case.

   c. Mr. Maxon spent five minutes in the Rock Room wiping a glass case with a cloth.

Nature Museum

2. What was Mrs. Kutsche doing when she noticed her ring was missing?

   a. Mrs. Kutsche was at her desk sorting through all of her extra paperwork.

   b. Mrs. Kutsche was in her office neatly filing her papers after lunch.

   c. Mrs. Kutsche worked in the Gem Room until late at night.

3. Where was Anya when her rock was taken?

   a. Anya first found her rock when she was on a tour of Spain three years ago.

   b. Anya spent two hours at a meeting in the Rock Room learning about geodes.

   c. Anya was busy learning about geodes for two hours.

Write four more questions with a friend that would help Detective Walker find out how, when, or where the thefts happened.

Name _____ Date _____

Why—Missing Ring

Make a sentence more interesting by telling why something happens. This allows a reader to understand the **cause** and **effect**.

Basic sentence:	Mr. Maxon put his keys on a table.
Better sentence:	Mr. Maxon put his keys on a table so he could clean a glass case.
Basic sentence:	Mrs. Kutsche kept the ring on her desk.
Better sentence:	Mrs. Kutsche kept the ring on her desk because she was going to show it to some coworkers.

The sentences below help to elaborate the cause and effect of why things happened. Write on the lines which of the basic elements—who, (did) what, where, why, or how—are in each sentence.

1. Anya kept a piece of quartz on her desk because it had broken off from a bigger piece of quartz. _____

2. Detective Walker looked for clues because he wanted to solve the crime.

   _____

3. Anya left her office to go to a meeting about geodes.

   _____

4. Mr. Maxon wrote a letter to Detective Walker to ask for help in solving the crimes.

   _____

5. Mrs. Kutsche looked for suspects in the museum because she wanted to know who took her ring. _____

6. Detective Walker realized who took the missing items because he found an important clue.

   _____

Work with a friend to create your own crime scene.
Make a list of causes and effects.

Putting It All Together

You can make your sentences more interesting and informative by telling *who, what, where, when,* and *how.*

Regular sentence: Anya walked into the room.

Super sentence: Anya, the museum's only rock expert, walked slowly into the meeting room early that morning to discuss the case with Detective Walker.

Detective Walker shared his findings with the people at the museum. Each of his sentences is missing one of the basic elements: *who, (did) what, where, when, why,* or *how.* Cross out each boxed element when you see it in the sentence. One word will be left.

1. Mr. Maxon, the manager of the Nature Museum, gently set his keys on a table in the Rock Room because he needed to clean one of the glass cases with a cloth.

who	did what	where	when	why	how

2. Mrs. Kutsche, the manager of the Gem Room, set the ring on her desk before lunch so that she could show it to some coworkers.

who	did what	where	when	why	how

3. Anya, the museum's rock expert, hunted carefully for two days, trying to find her missing piece of quartz.

who	did what	where	when	why	how

4. The naughty thief, who loves shiny objects, left clues in each room during the crimes because this species of thief sheds every season.

who	did what	where	when	why	how

 Write your own interesting and informative sentences with a friend to explain *who, what, where, when, why,* and *how* the keys, ring, and piece of quartz were taken by the thief.

Name _____ Date _____

Reveal the Mood

Tone is the writer's attitude or mood about the subject or topic. The writer's tone can be funny, serious, persuasive, happy, and so on.

Match each sentence to the tone it expresses.

___ **1.** disappointed   **a.** That's why we should all work hard to conserve energy.

___ **2.** happy   **b.** My projects never win at the science fair even though I work so hard on them.

___ **3.** funny   **c.** Every country on earth should do everything they can to prevent pollution.

___ **4.** serious   **d.** I can't believe I got an Honorable Mention!

___ **5.** technical   **e.** After I glued part A onto part B, I inserted the cotter pin.

___ **6.** persuasive   **f.** The first time I tried this, I ended up with spaghetti in my hair!

Circle the letter of the word that describes the tone of the paragraph below.

7. I never quite know what to do when teachers tell us we are going to have a science fair. First, they say we need to pick a project. The good experiments like exploding volcanoes and twisting tornadoes were all done last year. So what's left? Then, they make us do research. That means a trip to the library and filling out those index cards with our research, which always get mixed up. Couldn't we just use notebook paper? Then, there's the display. Playing soccer is easy, but writing on a poster board with a marker is hard. I detest science fairs!

    a. funny   **b.** serious   **c.** persuasive   **d.** frustrated   **e.** happy

Discuss with a friend what mood you'd like to set in a story. Using a subject that you've both experienced, write a paragraph using words that set the tone and have your friend do the same.

Name _____ Date _____

Your Experiences

Personal narratives tell about your experiences. To write a compelling personal narrative, you need to choose an unforgettable experience or an event that made an impression on you. Personal narratives are fairly short and describe only one experience.

The personal narrative below is from *Black Beauty*. It is written from the horse's point of view. What did Black Beauty learn from this memorable lesson from his mother?

> There were six colts in the meadow besides me. I used to run with them and had great fun; we would all gallop together round and round the field. Sometimes we had rather rough play, for we would frequently bite and kick.
>
> One day, when there was a good deal of kicking, my mother whinnied to me to come to her, "I wish you to pay attention to what I am about to say. The colts who live here are very good colts, but they are cart-horse colts, and, of course, they have not learned manners. You have been well-bred and wellborn; your father has a great name in these parts, and your grandfather won the cup two years in a row at the Newmarket Races; your grandmother had the sweetest temper of any horse I have ever known, and I think you have never seen me kick or bite. I hope you will grow up gentle and good and never follow bad ways. Do your work with goodwill, lift your legs up high when you trot, and never kick or bite, even in play."
>
> —Anna Sewell

Write about a learning experience or vacation that was special for you and why it was special. Include what people said to you in quotations just as Black Beauty's mother did in the passage above.

Brainstorm ideas with a friend about what memorable experiences you've had. Choose one experience to write about. Be sure to include your thoughts and feelings about the event or persons involved.

Name _____ Date _____

Writing a Biography

A **biography** is the story of a person's life. It contains significant facts about a person's life. The facts are often used to form an opinion and conclusion about the person.

Think of someone you know and admire that you would like to write a biography about. It could be someone in your family, a friend or a neighbor. On a separate sheet of paper, write down the answers to the following questions about this person. Combine your answers to write a biography and conclude from your answers why you admire this person. Is this person good, honest, intelligent, kind?

1. Where and when was this person born?

2. What were the family and home of this person like?

3. Where did this person go to school?

4. What jobs has this person had?

5. What special interests, hobbies, sports, or crafts does this person enjoy?

6. What interesting things have happened to this person?

Discuss with a friend someone you both admire and would like to write a biography about. Answer the questions above and combine your answers. Based on your answers, write several sentences that tell the facts and your opinions about this person.

Name _____ Date _____

Writing an Autobiography

An **autobiography** is the story of your life that you write yourself. You can tell the entire story of your life or just the main events. No matter how long you make it, your autobiography should be interesting and communicate what makes you a unique person.

To help get you started through the journey of your life, answer the following questions on a separate sheet of paper.

1. What is your name?

2. What do you like to be called?

3. Where were you born?

4. Where do you live now and where have you lived before?

5. What school do you go to and what other schools have you attended?

6. What is you favorite subject? Why?

7. What are your favorite hobbies? Why?

8. What are you very good at doing?

9. How many brothers and sisters do you have?

10. Who are your friends and why are they special to you?

11. What are your dreams for your future?

12. What makes your family different from other families?

13. What are you grateful for in life?

Write descriptive sentences from your answers including important events and major influences. Combine these into a story about your life.

 Share your autobiography with a friend and discuss how your lives have been different.

Name _____ Date _____

And So, My Fellow Americans...

Speeches inform others about a topic and/or persuade them to view things in a certain way. We often think of speeches when we think of people running for political office, such as President of the United States. Political speeches are only one type of speech, however. Any time a person must speak in front of a group, he or she must prepare a speech.

The **purpose** of the speech must be clear for it to be effective. Are you trying to encourage people to vote for you? Are you trying to explain a cause that you believe in and have researched? Are you trying to convince people that it is important to save the whales?

Once you have your purpose in mind, you can build your speech around it using examples, reasons, steps, important statistics, a series of questions, a short history, or funny stories that show your point.

Begin and end your speech by clearly stating your **major point**.

Below are the last two paragraphs from John F. Kennedy's Inaugural Address on January 20, 1961. Look up and read this speech on the Internet or in the library. What do you think was the main point of the speech?

And so my fellow Americans... ask not what your country can do for you... ask what you can do for your country. My fellow citizens of the world... ask not what America will do for you, but what together we can do for the Freedom of Man.

Finally, whether you are citizens of America or citizens of the world, ask of us here the same high standards of strength and sacrifice which we ask of you. With a good conscience our only sure reward, with history the final judge of our deeds; let us go forth to lead the land we love, asking His blessing and His help, but knowing that here on earth God's work must truly be our own.

— *John F. Kennedy*

And So, My Fellow Americans... (continued from page 50)

It is also very important to think about who your target audience will be. Write your speech so *this* audience will understand it. Avoid using any words or ideas that this audience wouldn't understand.

The **time limit** of your speech may be determined by your audience or by the subject of your speech. Avoid being too wordy and dragging the speech on because your audience may lose interest. An effective speech requires a careful choice of words and needs to be direct.

Below is the first paragraph from Lincoln's Gettysburg Address, given November 19, 1863 on the battlefield near Gettysburg, Pennsylvania. Look up and read this speech on the Internet or in the library. Who do you think Lincoln's target audience was and why do you think his speech wasn't very long but still so effective?

> Four score and seven years ago, our fathers brought forth upon this continent a new nation: conceived in liberty, and dedicated to the proposition that all men are created equal.

> —Abraham Lincoln

Do some research with a friend on endangered animals. Choose animals that interest you and write speeches to convince someone why this animal should not disappear from the planet. Give your speeches to each other, to friends, and family. Remember that speeches are meant to be heard, so they must *sound* good as well as be well written. Have your friend turn away from you when you give your speech as if you were giving your speech on the radio. See what your friend thought about how it sounded.

Name _____ Date _____

Reasons Why

In a **persuasive paragraph**, the writer tries to persuade the reader to do something or to think in a certain way.

A dog follows you home from the park. Your mother has some worries about keeping the dog. Read the reasons she's worried and circle the letter of the sentence that might persuade your mother that keeping the dog won't be a problem.

1. "You cannot keep the dog because he might belong to someone else."
   a. I will put up "Found" signs around the neighborhood to see if someone recognizes him.
   b. He does not have a name tag or a collar, and he followed me home.
   c. I already named him Scout.

2. "You cannot keep the dog because you do not know how to take care of him."
   a. You can take care of him, and I'll just play with him.
   b. Taking care of a dog is easy.
   c. I'll go to the pet store and ask them how to take care of a dog.

3. "You cannot keep the dog because he will track dirt into the house."
   a. He does not smell any worse than my brother's shoes.
   b. I will spray the house whenever he smells bad.
   c. I will wipe off his paws before he comes into the house.

Write a persuasive paragraph telling a parent why you should be able to keep a lost dog. Use the sentences above to deal with his or her doubts and add your own reasons. Remember that a paragraph needs a topic sentence and a concluding sentence.

Think of a place you'd like to go on a vacation with a friend and your family. Write a persuasive paragraph with your friend telling why you both think you should go there.

Name _____ Date _____

Volcano Erupts!

Scientists often write descriptions of what they observe. They use words that give the most complete description possible.

Circle the best description of each insect.

1.

a. This bug has a black body

b. This insect has two wings, large eyes, six legs, and a black body.

c. This insect can fly.

2.

a. This insect has antennae.

b. This bug can walk.

c. This insect has six legs, small eyes, and antennae.

Pretend that you are scientists in Hawaii. A volcano has erupted on the other side of the island. You have gone to see it from a safe distance and observe what has happened in the air, on land, and in the sea.

Do some research with a friend about volcanoes on the Internet or at the library. Write a few sentences together about what your observations would be if you saw a volcano erupting. Be sure to describe how it looks in the air, on land, and in the sea.

Why You Should Read This Book

Have you read any good books lately? Or have you read one in the past year that was unusual, interesting, or exciting? When we discover a wonderful book, we like to share our opinions about it.

On a sheet of notebook paper, write the name and author of a book that you have read and enjoyed. Answer the following questions to organize your ideas. Your answers will help you write a **persuasive book report**.

1. What is the main idea, focus, or theme of your book?

2. Who is the central character of the book? How would you describe the physical, mental, and emotional characteristics of this person?

3. Are there other important characters in the story? Who are they and what do they do?

4. What makes this book so interesting or exciting?

5. Give one example of a scene that was outstanding. Write some of the details.

6. Who tells the story in the book, or who is the narrator?

7. What is the narrator's point of view? What can the narrator see and hear?

Write a report about the book you selected, using the information from your answers. The concrete details and specific examples in your answers will enable you to write a persuasive report about your book.

Look through newspapers and magazines with a friend to find book reviews. Read the reviews, then discuss how the questions above were answered.

　　Name _____ Date _____

How Would You Rate the Movie?

Whether you have been to the movie theater or rented a video to watch on television, all of us today are **movie critics**.

Think about a movie you have seen recently. How would you rate it?
Was it a great movie? Or was it just okay? Or maybe you thought it was really bad. How many stars would you give—four, three, two, or one?

Write a movie review telling what you
liked and didn't like about the movie.
Was it exciting? Did it make you laugh out loud
or make you cry? Was it scary?
Where did the story take place? Who were the main characters?
What was the movie about? Would you recommend it to others?
What was your favorite part of the movie?

with a friend　　Have a friend write a review about the same movie, then exchange your
reviews to see if you had the same opinion. Discuss the things you both liked
and disliked about the movie.

　　0-7424-1785-9 *After School Writing Activities*

Name _____ Date _____

The Reporter's "Five and One" Rule

All good **news reporters** follow the "Five and One" rule. "Five" refers to who, what, when, where, and why. The "one" refers to how. Answers to the "Five and One" rule give clear information that can be quickly understood in a newspaper or a news report on television.

Study this first sentence from a paragraph of a made-up newspaper sports article. *When she was young, the champion, Sarah Hughes, perfected the skill of ice skating by many hours of pratice because her dream was to win a gold medal at the Winter Olympics.* Many of these questions are answered in one sentence.

Write your own article, using the "Five and One" rule. Select a famous star, hero, or expert in the subject you have chosen. Answer the following questions.

1. Who is the star, hero, or expert you have chosen?

2. What does he or she do?

3. When did he or she begin to do the activity that made him or her famous? You can add any other detail.

4. Where was he or she born? Where does your person perform his or her activity? Where did he or she learn to be outstanding?

5. Why is this person different or outstanding? Why does your person like the activity? Why do you admire your person?

6. How did your person become famous? How does your person rank among others?

Write an article about a subject in your own town. Have a friend do the same and exchange stories. Check each other's story to make sure the "Five and One" rule questions were answered in the story.

Name _____ Date _____

Extra! Extra!

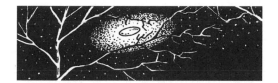

The facts in a **news story** answer the questions *who, what, when, where,* and sometimes, *why.* Read this news story.

Farmer Spots UFO

Sioux City, March 30—Thaddeus Briggs of Lone Pine Farm reported seeing an unidentified flying object in his corn field last night around 9 P.M. He described the UFO as a round object surrounded by a very bright white light. It hovered about 50 feet off the ground, emitting eerie sounds for about five minutes, and then sped off to the north.

"It was really a peculiar sight. I wasn't exactly frightened— just startled," Briggs stated.

1. On the lines below, fill in the facts from the news story above.

Who: _____

What: _____

When: _____

Where: _____

Newspaper reporters state only the facts of a story. A reporter may use an opinion or feeling if it is a quotation. Quotations are the exact words spoken by people.

2. Are there any opinions given in the story above? Write the opinion below and underline the expressive words used in the opinion.

_____

_____

Name _____ Date _____

Read Me!

Headlines state the main idea of a story in a few words. Here is another headline from the March 31 Sioux City paper.

Sioux City Disc Jockey Plays Music from Helicopter

Does this headline give you an idea for the *why* of the story on page 57? If so, fill in the reason below.

Why: _____

_____

The first paragraph of a news story is called the **lead**. The lead gives the important facts of a story. The lead should also be interesting and well written, so a reader will continue to read the news story. Write a lead paragraph for the Sioux City headline above. Make up specific facts that explain *who*, *what*, *when*, *where*, and *why*.

_____

_____

_____

_____

_____

_____

Write a news story based on one of the headlines below or make up a headline. Have a friend do the same.

New Science Museum to Open
Hunter Finds Strange Footprints
Tropical Storm Moves Inland

Use a good, factual lead paragraph that answers the "Five W" questions. Try to include a quotation that states an opinion. Read each other's stories. Check to see if *who*, *what*, *when*, *where*, and *why* were answered in the story.

Name _____ Date _____

Writing Ads for Products

Think of some of the most popular consumer products on the market today. Why are some brands of toothpaste, tennis shoes, soda pop, canned soup, fast foods, computer games, and types of music more successful than others?

What makes a product desirable to the general public? When marketing a product, advertising professionals ask *what is the purpose* of the product, *who* will want to buy it, and *why* people are going to want it. Then **advertisements** are created to sell the product.

One part of successful advertising is writing slogans that say the most with the fewest words.

Invent a product that you would use almost every day, something you would really enjoy. Think of something you think you need, such as a food, drink, tool, piece of clothing, accessory, or something fun, like a game. Perhaps you can think of a totally new product you would buy if you could.

What would it be? _____

What is the purpose of the product? _____

_____

_____

Who will want to buy it? _____

Why are they going to want to buy it? _____

_____

Write a slogan for this product that says the most using the fewest words.

When you're watching television with a friend, pay attention to the **jingles** in commercials. *(A jingle is a song with a catchy repetition.)* Pick your favorite jingle in a commercial and try to come up with a new one for the same product.

Name _____ Date _____

My Favorite Holiday

Everyone looks forward to holidays when family and friends get together for special traditions, food, and fun. Answer these questions on a separate sheet of paper.

What is your favorite holiday?

Explain why you selected this holiday by writing down the events that take place during your favorite holiday. Be **descriptive** with your details.

How long is your favorite holiday or the holiday season when you feel the good cheer of the holiday?

What music and entertainment do you enjoy during this holiday?

What kind of clothing or costumes do you wear?

What kinds of food are served during this time?

What other activities take place with your family or friends during this holiday?

Write a few paragraphs based on these answers to explain why this particular holiday is so special for you. Paint a picture with words so the reader can *see*, *hear*, and *smell* this holiday time.

Think of one memorable experience during your favorite holiday. It could be something like when you got a new bike for Christmas, when your favorite aunt traveled across the country to be with you for Thanksgiving, or the year you won the Halloween costume contest. Ask a friend about his or her special moment during a holiday. Write stories describing your special moments.

Maybe your friend was there during this special moment and you could both write a version of the same event.

greeting card   Name _____ Date _____

Thinking of You

Receiving a **greeting card** always makes you feel appreciated. Although greeting cards are popular during holidays and other special occasions, the surprise of getting a card for no particular occasion at all is especially nice.

Think of someone who would enjoy getting a special greeting from you.

What is the person's name? _____

What things has this person done that you appreciate? _____

_____

_____

_____

What has your special person done or said that affected you?

_____

_____

_____

Write a two- to four-line note to the person you chose. Include the nice things you listed above. When you finish, use a blank greeting card or a piece of note paper folded in half. If you use note paper, find an image in a magazine that you like and glue it on the front, or draw or paint a picture. Copy your lines on the inside and send it to the person you chose.

_____

_____

_____

_____

_____

_____

0-7424-1785-9 *After School Writing Activities*

Name _____ Date _____

Today I...

A **journal** or a **diary** is a daily record of personal experiences and observations. People write both facts and opinions in their journals.

Here are samples that could have come from the journals kept by two men during the famous Lewis and Clark expedition.

May 28, 1804

Tuesday

When I was hunting today, I came across a cave about 100 yards from the fork of a river on the south side. I went underground into the cave and saw a small spring. I stopped about 130 yards from the entrance because I didn't have a light. I would have gone farther if I had one. It is the most remarkable cave I've ever seen in my travels.

June 04, 1804

Saturday

We had good weather today so three hunters went out. The mast of our boat broke when I steered the boat too close to shore. The rope to the mast got caught in a limb of a sycamore tree and the mast broke very easily. We passed a creek on the south side of the river. We named it Nightingale Creek because a nightingale bird sang all last night. It is the first one we've heard on the river. This is beautiful land with oak, ash, black walnut, and hickory trees. Our hunters killed eight deer today and jerky was made this evening.

Write part of a diary about the time between coming home from school and going to bed for a week. Remember to write the day and date each time you write in your diary.

Discuss with a friend what each of you has done in the last seven days. Pick one day where you spent part of it with each other. Where were you? What did you do? Both of you write a journal entry that tells four facts about that day. Be sure to begin by writing the day and date. Compare your accounts of that day.

The next time you go on a family trip or a field trip with your class, keep a journal of the events of the trip and your feelings during it.

Writing a Letter to a Friend

In a letter to a friend, you may include a **heading**, which shows the writer's address as well as the date. The **greeting** states who you're writing the letter to, and the **body** presents your message. The **closing** is the way you say goodbye. Your **signature** tells the person receiving the letter who wrote it. In a letter to a friend, you usually only use a first name in the greeting and the signature. Below is a sample of a letter to a friend.

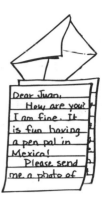

Tuesday, June 28

Dear Sergio,

    It was so good to see you at the park the other day. It's been such a long time since I've seen you. I've missed all of my old friends since my family moved. Have you seen our friend Suzanne lately? What's she up to?

    I'm having a few friends over for lunch next week. Would you like to come? Please let me know. I would love to see you again.

                  Fondly,

                  Lee

Write a letter to a friend or someone in your family that you haven't seen in awhile.

Find out if there are any groups or associations in your town that will set you up with a pen pal in another country. Another possibility is to exchange letters with a soldier who is stationed either in this country or overseas. Have a friend sign up too, and you will both enjoy writing to a new friend. You can share ideas as you write your letters and news when you get letters back.

Name _____ Date _____

Writing a Business Letter

A business letter is more formal and is written flush left, where the heading, inside address, greeting, body of letter, closing, and signature all begin at the left-hand margin.

The **greeting** is more formal than in a friendly letter, and includes the name and title of the person receiving the letter. If you don't know the name or title of the person, he or she can be addressed as *Dear Sir or Dear Madam, or To Whom It May Concern.* The greeting is followed by a colon (:). The **closing** is more formal as well. The most common closings are *Sincerely yours, Sincerely, Yours truly, or Cordially.* The **signature** usually has the writer's name handwritten beneath the closing, and then printed or typed below that. Below is a sample of a business letter.

222 Hampton St.
New York, NY 95602
September 30, 2002

Emmett & Gray Publishing Co.
41 Smythe St.
Marblehead, MA 46802

To Whom It May Concern:

I have not received the book *Life in the Ocean,* that I ordered from your company three weeks ago. I would appreciate it if you would let me know when it will be delivered.

Sincerely yours,

Gene Warren

Gene Warren

Write a business letter to a company that makes a food product, telling them why you like it. Follow the guidelines to format your letter. The company's address may be on the label or box.

Write a make-believe letter to a business with a friend. It could be about a certain product that you both like or one that you'd like to complain about.

Name _____ Date _____

Sunset

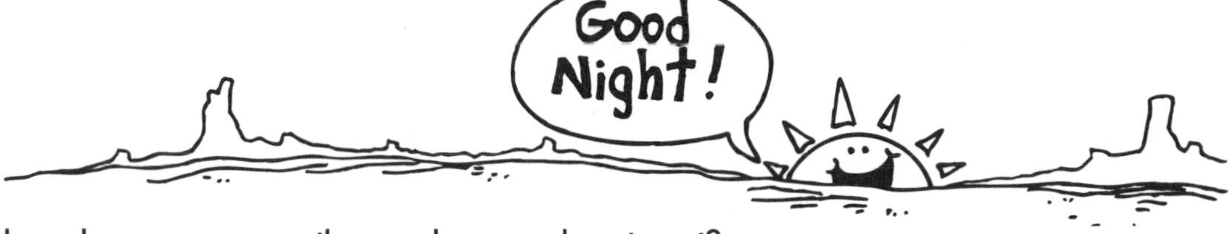

How do you suppose the sun knows when to set?

_____

_____

_____

Why do you think the sun is often drawn with a happy face?

_____

_____

_____

Why are the colors in a sunset different every time you see one?

_____

_____

_____

Describe a sunset you have experienced.

_____

_____

_____

_____

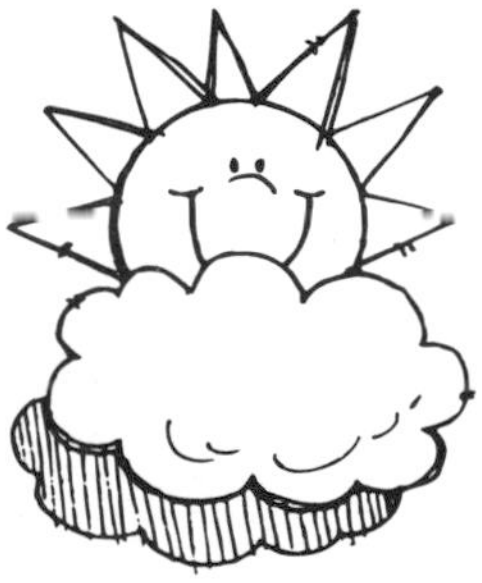

Name _____ Date _____

What Does the Future Hold?

Can you think of something you are doing today that could have an effect on the future? Describe it.

_____

_____

Describe three things you are helping to change for the better, whether about yourself or the environment.

_____

_____

_____

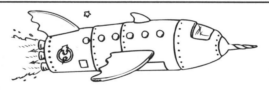

If you could travel in time, what message would you give to a child living thirty years in the future? Why?

_____

_____

Describe what you think the future will be like in twenty years.

_____

_____

_____

_____

Name _____ Date_____

What Is an Archaeologist?

Why do you think the Egyptian pyramids were built?

_____

_____

_____

How do you think the ancient Egyptians were able to build the pyramids without modern equipment?

_____

_____

_____

What might explain why pyramids were built in the triangular shape?

_____

_____

_____

What does an archaeologist do?

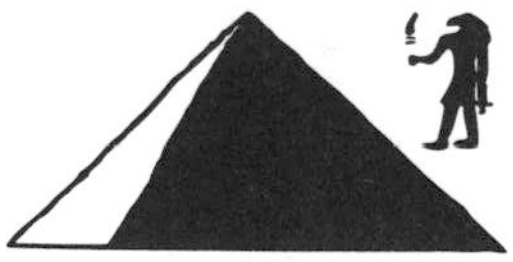

_____

_____

_____

_____

_____

_____

_____

Name _____ Date _____

Who Likes Music?

What are three reasons why some people are good musicians and others are not?

_____

_____

_____

Why do you think people enjoy singing with others?

_____

_____

If you could master any musical instrument, what would you choose and why?

_____

_____

_____

What do you like most about music?

_____

_____

_____

_____

_____

_____

Name _____ Date _____

Three Wishes

• What do people mean when they wish someone good luck?

_____

_____

_____

• What is meant by *superstition?*_____

_____

_____

_____

• Why are some things considered to be lucky?

_____

_____

_____

• If you had three wishes, what would they be and why?

_____

_____

_____

_____

_____

0-7424-1785-9 *After School Writing Activities*

Name _____ Date _____

Weather Watch

- What are the most obvious changes to the environment between summer and winter?

  _____

  _____

- Why do you think some people enjoy warm temperatures more than cold?

  _____

  _____

- Name four activities that are most often done in the winter and four most often done in the summer.

  _____

  _____

- Describe your favorite season of the year and why.

  _____

  _____

  _____

  _____

  _____

  _____

  _____

Name _____ Date _____

Where in the World?

Why do many people enjoy traveling to warm climates?

_____

_____

_____

What location in the United States do you think is the most popular place to go on vacation? Why?

_____

_____

_____

Describe what it feels like to have nothing to do.

_____

_____

Describe the best place you have ever gone for a vacation.

_____

_____

_____

_____

_____

Name _____ Date _____

Why Do We Shake Hands?

What are some different ways people say hello to their pets?

_____

_____

_____

How do animals say hello to each other? _____

_____

_____

_____

People have many different ways of saying hello to their family and friends. Give

three examples. _____

_____

_____

_____

Why do many adults shake hands when they say hello?

_____

_____

_____

_____

_____

_____

_____

72
0-7424-1785-9 *After School Writing Activities*

Name _____ Date _____

Long Life

Why do you think people believe that having a pet helps you to stay healthy?

_____

_____

Why are people living longer today that they did in the last century?

_____

_____

_____

In what countries do you think people live the longest? Why do you think this is so?

_____

_____

_____

Why do you think most humans live longer than most animals?

_____

_____

_____

_____

_____

Name _____ Date _____

Splash Down

What is your favorite thing to do in or with water?

_____

_____

_____

Where do rain and snow come from? _____

_____

_____

_____

What would change if we did not have oceans?

_____

_____

_____

Describe ten tasks for which water is a necessity.

_____

_____

_____

_____

_____

_____

_____

Name _____ Date _____

Realistic Fiction

Realistic fiction tells a story that could actually happen. Read the following paragraph and cross out the sentences that you don't believe are realistic.

The wind blew strongly against the window of Gurney's bedroom. Inside, Gurney was getting ready to go to bed. He put on his pajamas and said his prayers. He climbed into bed and turned off the lamp. A bright light shone through his window. Gurney jumped up to see what caused the light. Outside the window he saw a large, glowing spacecraft with green and blue flashing lights. Gurney put his clothes back on and prepared to go outside. After he tied his shoes, he ran down the stairs faster than a speeding train, and opened the front door. His pet lizard, Sammy, asked Gurney,

"What's wrong Gurney? You look upset." Gurney went outside. He stood on the porch and looked at the lawn. He saw that the door of the spacecraft was about to open. He jumped over the roof of the house, picked up a one-ton rock from the backyard, and jumped back to face the space invader. When the door opened, his mother and father were inside. "Gurney, you're awake," they said, "Come inside and look at our new minivan camper."

Think of an event that actually happened to you or someone you know. Now organize the story in the order that it happened. Write a fictional story based on this real event. Remember to include who the story is about, and how, where, when, and why the story happened.

Name _____ Date _____

Science Fiction

Science fiction is a type of fictional writing that uses current ideas in science to imagine what life might be like in the future. The story is still an imaginary tale, but there might be parts of it that could be true many years from now.

Some of the topics you find in a science fiction stories include time travel, space travel, aliens, and the effects of technology. Science fiction writers often set their stories in the future in order to talk about the world in which they live. For example, Mary Shelley's 19th-century novel *Frankenstein* is a story about a scientist who builds a monster out of human body parts. As well as wanting to tell a good story, Shelley also wanted to warn readers that science could create both good and bad things.

It was with these feelings that I began the creation of a human being. As the minuteness of the parts formed a great hindrance to my speed, I resolved, contrary to my first intention, to make the being of a gigantic stature, that is to say, about eight feet in height, and proportionably large.

—*Mary Shelley*

Other science fiction writers, like Jules Verne, simply liked to create adventure stories that featured rocket ships and submarines. Verne wrote the science fiction novel *20,000 Leagues Under the Sea* about Captain Nemo and his submarine, *The Nautilus*, before submarines were a part of everyday life.

It became necessary to renew the atmosphere of our prison, and no doubt the whole in the submarine boat. That gave rise to a question in my mind. How would the commander of this floating dwelling-place proceed?

—*Jules Verne*

0-7424-1785-9 *After School Writing Activities*

Name _____ Date _____

Science Fiction (continued from page 76)

Another science fiction writer, H.G. Wells, wrote adventure stories about future warfare. Wells' novel *The War of the Worlds* was an adventure story about an attack on Earth by invaders from Mars. No matter what weapons the people of Earth used, the invaders could not be stopped. Earth was saved in the end, however, when tiny bacteria made the Martian invaders get sick and die.

Two large dark-colored eyes were regarding me steadfastly. The mass that framed them, the head of the thing, was rounded, and had, one might say, a face. There was a mouth under the eyes, the lipless brim of which quivered and panted, and dropped saliva. The whole creature heaved and pulsated convulsively. A lank tentacular appendage gripped the edge of the cylinder, another swayed in the air.

—H.G. Wells

Write your own science fiction story. Make the story take place in the future. Draw a picture that could be on the cover.

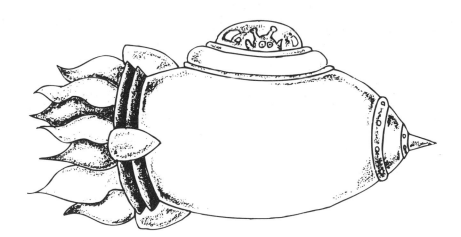

 Create a scene that takes place in the future. Imagine that you and your friend are adults. What will cars look like? How will food be different? Will the world be a better place? How? What will be some of the new inventions that you and your friend will use? Here's a sample title for a story: "My Best Friend's Mom Is a Robot."

0-7424-1785-9 *After School Writing Activities*

Name _____ Date _____

All the World's a Stage

Drama is a story that is told by actors. The ancient Greeks used drama to tell stories about kings, rulers, and the Greek gods. These plays were either comedies or tragedies. A **comedy** is a play that makes people laugh. A **tragedy** is a play with an ending that features the downfall of the hero or heroes. Perhaps the most famous Greek tragedy is Oedipus Rex (Ed-i-pus Rex), which tells the story of a king whose pride results in tragic deeds. During the Renaissance of the 16th century, English writers like William Shakespeare and Christopher Marlowe wrote many comedies, as well as historical and tragic dramas.

In Italy in the late 1500s, ancient Greek plays were discovered that were sung by the actors. The Italians decided to try writing musical dramas, too. This musical drama came to be known as **opera**. Many of these operas were based on ancient Greek stories. Operas became very popular in Europe with both rich and poor audiences, and are still popular today!

Write your own comedy or a tragedy based on the explanations above.

Think of a story that happened to you or someone you know. Write down the events in the order that they happened. Think of some of your favorite songs. Use these songs to help tell your story. You have just written a musical! Now perform your musical for your family and friends.

Name _____ Date _____

All the World's a Stage (continued from page 78)

The words that actors speak to each other are called **dialogue**. A *soliloquy* is a device used in drama to tell the audience what a character is really thinking. When an actor delivers a soliloquy, they speak directly to the audience and not to the other actors.

The following soliloquy tells you a lot about the character. What do you know about this character?

To go to school or to stay home, that's what I can't decide.
What difference does it make if I get out of bed or not?
It's always the same old thing day after day. If I stay in bed, I
won't have to take the quiz today that I didn't study for last night.
If I sleep, I might have a nice dream. But, then again, I might have
that bad dream again where I go to school wearing nothing but my
underwear. Why didn't I study last night? Oh, no. Mom's calling me.
I guess I'd better get dressed, eat breakfast, and go to school.

1. Is the character a good student? Support your answer with a sentence from the soliloquy.

_____

2. Why does the character eventually decide to go to school? Support your answer.

_____

3. What is the character's biggest fear? Support your answer.

_____

To understand how a drama is created, ask your parents how they first met. Ask them to remember details about what they said to each other, how they dressed, and how they acted. Write down what you learned using dialogue. Include instructions on how to read it. Tell their story in a way that is realistic. Act it out with your friend.

Name _____ Date _____

Seeing with Your Ears

In 1920, Pittsburgh radio station KDKA broadcast election results. After that, hundreds of radio stations were built and thousands of Americans bought radios for their homes.

Radio became even more popular when it broadcast a boxing match between Jack Dempsey and Georges Carpentier in 1921. Baseball games were broadcast into nearly three million homes.

As radios became more common, the station owners had to compete with each other for listeners. They began broadcasting dramas written specifically for radio audiences. Because there were no pictures, the **radio dramas** relied on narrators and sound effects to create pictures in the listener's mind. One of the most popular radio dramas was *Amos 'N Andy*, which began in 1929.

In the 1930s and 1940s, radio enjoyed what is known as its "Golden Age." During this period, radio drama was very popular. Homes across America tuned in every week to hear radio comedies such as *Fibber McGee and Molly* and *The Fred Allen Show*, and dramatic shows such as *The Green Hornet* and *The Shadow*.

Look up a script of one of the old radio dramas mentioned above on the Internet or at the library. Read it and write your own episode for the show following the same format and story line.

Select your favorite story to use as a radio play. Before you begin, bring together all the different items you will need to create your drama's sound effects. Write a script for your radio play. Perform and record your play and "broadcast" it to your family, friends, or classroom. You may want to borrow tapes of old radio drama broadcasts from your local library to help you plan your recording.

Name _____ Date _____

The Shadow Knows...

One of the most popular radio programs of all times was *The Shadow*. It always began with the Shadow asking in a deep voice, "Who knows what evil lurks in the hearts of men?" He then answered the question, "The Shadow knows!" The actor portraying the Shadow would then perform a terrifying laugh, which has become among the best-remembered **radio drama** lines of all time.

Based on a series of books by Maxwell Grant, the radio series told the adventures of a man "who could cloud men's minds so that they could not see him." Because criminals could not see him, the Shadow was able to capture criminals and solve mysteries without ever revealing his true identity.

Who was the Shadow? In the early novels the Shadow was Kent Allard who sometimes impersonated Lamont Cranston, "wealthy young man about town." By the late 1940s Cranston took over the identity of the Shadow with no mention of Allard. Lamont Cranston befriends Margo Lane who knows that Cranston is the Shadow, but tells no one and helps him to solve crimes.

How did the Shadow learn to cloud men's minds? As a World War I pilot and spy, he had the unusual ability to see in the dark. He wound up on a mountain in Tibet, where he learned an ancient secret of hypnotizing people so that they could not see him.

Pick one of your favorite crime fighters from a cartoon or a comic book and write a couple of catchy opening lines for this character's radio drama.

Write a ten-minute radio script with a friend that features your own crime fighter. Give your hero a special power that no one else has. Your crime fighter will need a sidekick, a person who has no special powers but knows the true identity of your hero.

Name _____ Date _____

Rip Van Winkle

The main purpose of **historical fiction** is to give the reader information about a certain time period, person, or event in history. In historical fiction you can include people who actually lived and have them do things they did not really do or go to places where they did not really go. You can make up people and have them do things and go to places that actually existed, or you can make yourself a time traveler and take part in history any way you like!

Read the passage from *Rip Van Winkle*. Then, answer the questions below.

At the foot of these fairy mountains, the voyager may have descried the light smoke curling up from a village, whose shingle-roofs gleam among the trees, just where the blue tints of the upland melt away into the fresh green of the nearer landscape. It is a little village of great antiquity, having been founded by some of the Dutch colonists, in the early times of the province, just about the beginning of the government of the good Peter Stuyvesant, (may he rest in peace!) and there were some of the houses of the original settlers standing within a few years, built of small yellow bricks brought from Holland, having latticed windows and gable fronts, surmounted with weather-cocks.

In that same village, and in one of these very houses (which, to tell the precise truth, was sadly time-worn and weather-beaten), there lived many years since, while the country was yet a province of Great Britain, a simple good-natured fellow of the name of Rip Van Winkle.

—*Washington Irving*

1. What parts of this passage do you think are historical facts? _____

_____

2. What do you think is the fictional part of this story? _____

_____

Name _____ Date _____

Rip Van Winkle (continued from page 82)

Writing historical fiction requires some research. Once you decide on what period of history you would like to use in your story, you will need to find out more about the people, the time period, and the events that are connected to your topic.

Here are some important things you might include when you write your story:

☆ clothing   ☆ famous people of that era
☆ ways of communicating   ☆ methods of transportation
☆ types of food   ☆ ways of speaking
☆ types of houses   ☆ type of government
☆ important events of that era

Ask a friend to help you choose a person, a place, an event, or a time period of history that you would like to explore. Gather some information for the story from books, films, magazines, or the Internet. Make lists of the information you discover in each of the categories mentioned above. Compose your story together from your lists of information and use your imagination!

Name _____ Date _____

Live Theater: On TV!

Fifty years ago, TV was much different than it is today. Many of the shows we watch today are videotaped or filmed. This means that actors and production people can redo scenes if they make a mistake. If a mistake was made on live TV in the early days, it was broadcast for the entire country to see.

The 1950s are known as "The Golden Age of Television." During this time, actors, writers, and directors worked very quickly to produce shows that were known for their high quality.

Your local newspaper has asked you to be a TV critic. What are your favorite TV shows? Write down why you like these shows. Remember to discuss the characters, the stories, and the acting. What are your favorite episodes and why?

Some things to consider in writing your review:
1. Why is this a good show?
2. Are the stories original?
3. Are there any other shows like it?
4. What type of audience do you think would like the show best?

Watch a rerun of an old black-and-white TV show with a friend and compare it to a new TV show. Keep in mind that you should compare comedies to comedies and compare dramas to dramas. Write down your answers to the following questions on a separate sheet of paper.

1. How are the shows different? How are they the same?
2. Which show did you like better? Why?
3. How has time changed the way TV shows are written?
   Is this good or bad, in your opinion?

 0-7424-1785-9 *After School Writing Activities*

Writing for Television

When you write for television, like writing a play, you have to add **stage directions**. Stage directions describe the setting where the scene takes place, and tell the actors what to do or how to say their lines. Stage directions appear in parentheses and are not meant to be said out loud. Here are some examples:

ACT 1, SCENE 1

(The train has just pulled into the station. MARGE and BUCK are standing on the platform with their suitcases. MOTHER is behind them, weeping.)

MOTHER: (dabbing her eyes with a handkerchief) Goodbye darlings. May the angels watch over you. I'll join you in a week.
BUCK: (hugging her) Goodbye, Mama.
MARGE: (between sobs) Why can't you come with us, Mama? I can't go without you.

Some important points to remember when writing your script:

- Realistic dialogue is very important because the characters are telling the story to the audience.
- Dialogue does not have to be in quotation marks because the character is identified at the beginning of each speaking part.
- Remember to imagine your play on stage and write clear stage directions when necessary.
- Acts are like chapters in a book.

Write a new episode for your favorite television show. Before you begin, write down some details about the characters and the settings. Decide what you want your characters to do in this episode. Continue the theme of a recent episode you saw? Create a whole new situation.

Name _____ Date _____

The Elf of the Rose

A fantasy story is a story that could never happen. Such stories contain events, ideas, or even imaginary worlds that do not, and cannot, exist. Fantasy stories often have magical aspects or include journeys, quests, or dreams. They may have characters such as elves, fairies, leprechauns, wizards, giants, or talking animals. It's fun to write fantasy stories because your imagination can really take off!

Below is a passage from *The Elf of the Rose,* a fairy tale written in 1872 by Hans Christian Andersen.

In the midst of a garden grew a rose-tree, in full blossom, and in the prettiest of all the roses lived an elf. He was such a little wee thing, that no human eye could see him. Behind each leaf of the rose he had a sleeping chamber. He was as well formed and as beautiful as a little child could be, and had wings that reached from his shoulders to his feet. Oh, what sweet fragrance there was in his chambers! And how clean and beautiful were the walls! For they were the blushing leaves of the rose.

During the whole day he enjoyed himself in the warm sunshine, flew from flower to flower, and danced on the wings of the flying butterflies.

—Hans Christian Andersen

Imagine what it would be like to…

travel on stardust

discover a magical world in a forest

meet a wizard

Write a fantasy story using one of the ideas above.

with a friend

Brainstorm with a friend to come up with your own fantasy story. Create the impossible in your story. Have your main character reach a goal, have an adventure, or learn an important truth. Help your readers to escape everyday life by entering your world of fantasy!

Two Guys Walk into Study Hall

Everybody knows at least one joke. This is a classic "Knock, Knock" joke.

"Knock, knock."
"Who's there?"
"Dwayne."
"Dwayne, who?"
"Dwayne the bathtub, I'm dwoning."

Puns are another type of joke. Puns rely on words with more than one meaning or words that are mispronounced on purpose. The following story ends with a pun.

There was a Wizard who worked in a factory. He enjoyed his job except when mischievous workers would take advantage of his good nature and steal his parking spot. The workers continued to do this until he put up the following sign: "This parking space belongs to the Wizard... Violators will be **toad**."

1. Write down what you think is the funniest joke you have ever heard. Explain what makes the joke so funny.

2. Who is your favorite comic? Write down why you think he or she is so funny.

3. Write your own standup comedy routine. Try to use jokes that everyone can understand.

Obtain a copy of the text to the Bud Abbott and Lou Costello baseball comedy routine "Who's on First?" and present it with a friend to your class, friends, or parents. What makes the routine so funny?

You Think You're Funny?

A **joke** can be a story that is told in a careful sequence. It usually ends with a punch line, which is the unexpected twist that makes the listener laugh. Read the comic strip below and pay attention to the order of events.

You Think You're Funny? (continued from page 88)

A. Can you tell the joke on page 88 entirely in words? Write a paragraph about it. Be sure to write the joke in the correct order of events. Using words such as *then* and *finally* help keep the order clear.

_____

_____

_____

_____

_____

_____

B. If you put the following sentences in sequence, you will get a joke.
Number the sentences in order. Then write them in a paragraph.

_____ He takes a sip and screams, "This coffee tastes like mud."

_____ A man goes into a diner and orders a cup of coffee.

_____ The waiter says, "Well, it was ground this morning."

_____ Hey, did you hear this one?

_____

_____

_____

_____

Work together to write a joke. Make sure that your story leads up to a funny punch line and that the punch line comes as a surprise.

Name _____ Date _____

Digging a Hole to Arizona

A **tall tale** is a greatly exaggerated story. Many times, tall tales feature heroes who accomplish amazing deeds or are responsible for accidentally creating some of the land forms we see today. For example, the tall tale cowboy hero Pecos Bill was said to have ridden on a cyclone (a tornado) in order to try and tame it. He lassoed the cyclone and dug his spurs into the ground. The cyclone dragged Pecos Bill from Colorado to Arizona. Pecos Bill's spurs digging into the ground created the Grand Canyon.

Another tall tale character is Paul Bunyan, a giant lumberjack who owned the equally giant Babe the Blue Ox. Paul Bunyan could cut down all the trees in a forest with one swing of his giant axe. The Paul Bunyan stories are known for their use of *hyperbole*, which is an extravagant exaggeration. For example, one Paul Bunyan story is about a winter that is so cold that the lumberjacks cannot speak because the words freeze in the air and fall to the ground the minute they are spoken.

Create your own tall tale hero. See if you can make your hero responsible for a river that runs through your town, a mountain, or large hill nearby. You could also make your hero responsible for the oceans and the shape of the continents.

Complete the following statements with a hyperbole. Ask a friend to do the same and see what you both come up with for the same beginnings.

1. Last night it was so cold, _____

2. My father's car is so fast, _____

3. My best friend is so smart, _____

4. My dog can jump so high, _____

5. My radio played so loud, _____

0-7424-1785-9 *After School Writing Activities*

Name _____ Date _____

Unfairy Tales

A **parody** is a long joke that makes fun of a story, poem, or song by imitating it. A parody changes parts of the story or poem to make the reader laugh. For example, Laura Cecil wrote a parody called *The Frog Princess.* In her version of a traditional tale, a prince, who is forced to marry an ugly frog finds out his bride is really a beautiful princess.

A parody of another classic fairy tale might go something like this:

The prince was disappointed. He had put the glass slipper on the foot of every woman in the kingdom. Each time he found that the women's feet were either too big or too small. He was tired of looking at feet all day. He wished some people would take better care of their feet. He had seen too many bunions and blisters. He told his helpers (his "foot" servants!) to tell the women that they couldn't put high-fashion footwear on yucky feet. "Please," thought the prince, "my kingdom for a woman who looks good in glass footwear!"

I. What story is parodied?
   a. Snow White and the Seven Dwarfs
   b. Sleeping Beauty
   c. Cinderella

2. Rewrite one of your favorite fairy tales to create a parody.

Pick a favorite movie, television show, song, or story. Now write a parody of it. Try to make it as funny as you can. Read it to your classmates or family members

Name _____ Date _____

Myths

A **myth** attempts to explain what is not understood. The ancient Greeks, Romans, Africans, and Native Americans invented many myths to explain why things happen. The myth of the Norse character Thor, for example, explains how thunder is made. When Thor strikes with his giant hammer, he creates thunder.

Another myth is about how the Roman god Apollo drove a chariot that dragged the sun across the sky every day. This is how the sun rose and set every day. Apollo's son Phaeton asked his dad if he could borrow the family chariot for a day. Apollo explained that it wasn't easy controlling his horses as they made the steep climb up to the noon hour and the steep decline toward sunset. Knowing about the great horsepower of his dad's chariot made Phaeton want to drive it even more. Finally, Apollo said yes. Phaeton grabbed the horses' reins and took off. When he couldn't control the horses, they dragged the sun too close to the earth, burning the ground and creating deserts. Then they flew wildly into the sky, far away from the earth, which created Earth's colder climates.

Write your own myth about something you could not understand without science. For example, you could write about why the moon sometimes shines during the day. Be creative!

Look up Native American myths on the Internet or at the library with a friend. Work with your friend to write your own myth about North America.

0-7424-1785-9 *After School Writing Activities*

Name _____ Date _____

Legends

A **legend** is a story that has been passed down through history. Many times, a legend will exaggerate what really happened. Legends may include parts from an original story changed to include amazing abilities or events. The legendary hero of "The Ballad of John Henry," for example, is a man of incredible strength. John Henry is so strong, he can swing his nine-pound hammer harder and faster than a steel drill.

The characters or stories of legend may also be real. Many legends have been passed down about Davy Crockett and Daniel Boone. Some of the stories that we know about these men, however, only happened in the imaginations of the writers who made them up. For example, we can be certain that neither of these men killed bears with their bare hands.

"FATHER, I CANNOT TELL A LIE..."

Other legends that concern fictional actions by historical people may be believable. That doesn't mean that these actions actually happened. The stories of George Washington chopping down a cherry tree and throwing a silver dollar across the Delaware River are two popular legends.

Do some research on the Internet or at the library on a popular legendary figure, such as those mentioned above. Write your own legend about him or her from your findings. Be sure to include some exaggerated tales.

Pick a person from history, sports, or entertainment. Write a legend about the person's special abilities or accomplishments. Feel free to exaggerate as much as possible to make your legend entertaining. Give your legend an interesting title. For example, you might title your story, "The Legend of Abraham Lincoln and the Overdue Library Book."

Name _____ Date _____

The Moral of the Story

A **fable** is a short story that teaches the reader a lesson. The lesson is called the **moral** of the story. The characters in fables are often animals or elements of nature who act like humans.

The following is one of Aesop's Fables. It is called *The North Wind and the Sun.*
The North Wind and the Sun argued as to which was the most powerful, and
agreed that he should be declared the victor who could first strip a
traveling man of his clothes.

The North Wind first tried his power and blew with
all his might, but the stronger his blasts, the closer
the traveler wrapped his cloak around him, until at
last, resigning all hope of victory, the Wind called upon
the Sun to see what he could do.

The Sun suddenly shone out with all his warmth.
The Traveler no sooner felt his warm rays than he
took off one garment after another, and at last, fairly
overcome with heat, took off his cloak, and cooled
himself in a stream.

1. What is a good moral for the fable?
   a. Persuasion is better than force.
   b. Might makes right.
   c. People are stronger than the wind.
   d. Don't count your chickens before they are hatched.

Write your own fable. Begin by deciding what lesson you want to teach.
Invent animal characters to tell your fable.

Name _____ Date _____

Snow Days

One _____ you wake up to discover that it

has snowed _____ overnight. The snow looks _____ and _____

from your _____ window. You run down the _____ to eat a breakfast of

_____, _____, and _____. Then, you and _____ race

to get ready to _____.

Outside the air is _____ and _____. The snow crunches like

_____ beneath your _____. Your _____ boots sink

_____ into the _____ snow. Oh, how _____ the world looks!

From down the _____, you _____ your friend calling _____ to

you. _____ wants to build a _____. You _____ your parents and

run over as fast as _____. It will _____ a lot of _____

to build one of those.

After working _____ all _____, the _____ is done. It stands

_____ _____ tall and is bigger than your _____. Now you feel

_____ and very hungry. It is time for _____.

_____ mother has made some _____ and _____ cookies just

for you. She thinks your project looks very _____. After you have _____

eating, she takes a _____ of you standing by it. It has been a _____ day.

Best of all, _____ says there will be _____ more _____

of snow tomorrow!

My State Fair

It is time for the _____ state fair to _____. _____ are taking some of their best _____ from their _____ garden to show. Aunt _____ is entering her famous _____ jelly and _____ pie. Your cousin _____ has been working on a _____ project to be shown in the youth area.

_____ year, your family plans to _____ a good time at the fair. There are _____ things to eat, like _____ and _____. Homemade _____ and _____ are a real treat!

There is so much to _____ and _____. In the _____ are _____ carnival rides and some _____ games to try. Everyone tries to win _____ by _____. The smell of _____ fills the air. Children ride _____ cars and the _____ . A _____ band plays _____ while people _____. Everyone has a _____ time.

Soon it is time for the _____ eating contest. Last year's winner ate _____ _____. Later there will be a _____ race and a _____ pulling contest.

Nearby in the _____, farmers and 4-H members have brought their _____ and horses to show. My favorite animals at the fair are the _____. I think they are _____ because _____.

Name _____ Date _____

The Bird Feeder

Our new principal is _____. The _____ found out _____

likes birds. We are _____ a new bird feeder for _____.

We _____ make it out of _____ and glass. It will be able to hold

_____ of bird food. When we are _____, we _____ it outside

our principal's office window in the small _____ tree. _____ can look

at it everyday.

Our new principal _____ it. Each day _____ birds come to

_____ there. On _____ we saw some _____ and

_____. On several days _____ and _____ came. Maybe we

will even see a _____ or a _____ later this _____.

In _____, a furry _____ decided to visit the _____.

_____ ate a lot of the _____. Those must be _____. We put

some _____ out for the _____ to _____ so _____

would not destroy _____ bird feeder.

It was a _____ winter. We used _____ of bird seed. We are

_____ another feeder for next _____. Maybe _____ birds will

come. I guess you could say our _____ is for the birds.

Garden Time

Spring is _____ and you _____ to plant a garden in the _____ near the _____. Your teacher, _____, has given _____ class packets of _____ seeds to _____. This is your _____ garden, so you want it to be _____ and _____.

First, you _____ a _____ spot. Then you _____ the soil. Your _____ gives you a rake, a shovel, and a hoe to _____. At first, the soil is _____ because it is _____. After a while it gets _____. You use a _____ to make _____.

Then you _____ the packet of _____ and _____ seeds. Next, you _____ to plant some _____ and some _____. Your favorite _____ is _____. You save some _____ for a _____ of that, too. When you are finished, you can see _____.

Your _____ wants to help you _____. Maybe _____ could _____ the _____. That is a very _____ job. It is _____ to have some help.

Finally, you _____ the _____ to water everything. When you are finished, you must _____ up the mess by _____. Your family thinks your garden is very _____. _____ says, "_____."

In a few _____, the _____ begin to sprout. You can almost _____ how they are going to _____. What a _____ project!

Stepping Back in Time

You are _____ with your _____ on a tour of _____ castles in Ireland. Your favorite part is the _____. As you start to leave, a _____ doorway catches your _____. You trip and _____ your head on an old _____.

When you awake, you are _____. Night has _____ but you still _____ people talking. Nearby you smell _____ food and _____. People dressed in _____ clothes walk by you. Somehow, you have _____ back in time! You _____ to explore some of the _____ before the _____ notice you. You don't want to end up in the _____.

The _____ of the castle are made of _____ and mortar. A _____ staircase _____ to the _____ of the tower. From here you can see the _____ and the _____ where the _____ stands. The knights' horses are _____ in the stable by the _____.

In case of _____, the _____ can raise the drawbridge and _____ the _____ inside. Across the _____ a _____ keeps watch for _____. Tonight all is _____.

The Lost Planet

You are traveling on a _____ space ship to the planet _____.
You have been told the planet is very _____. The surface of the planet looks like
_____. There is no _____, _____ or _____ there.
You are hoping to see _____.

Your ship has _____ three boxes of _____, some cans of
_____ and _____ pounds of _____. Your crew members'
names are _____, _____, and _____. They are all very
_____ space travelers. This is your _____ trip as captain of the crew.

As the ship _____ near the planet, you see _____ and
_____. You wonder if you should _____ . Instead, you decide to
_____ and turn on the _____ to enter the planet's _____.

Upon landing, the space ship breaks a _____ and must _____ before
you can _____. Far away you see some _____ mountains. You decide to
_____ the region. If you ever get _____, you will _____.

0-7424-1785-9 *After School Writing Activities*

Name _____ Date _____

Story Starter

When I was in the pumpkin patch with my family to pick out our pumpkin for Halloween, a funny-shaped pumpkin asked me ...

If I could change the results of something I saw on the news in the past year, it would be...

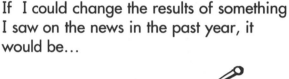

If I were a farmer, I would grow _____ (a crop) and have _____ (animals) because...

When we were camping on the beach, we...

Name _____ Date _____

Story Starter

One day, while petting my dog, he licked me and we suddenly switched identities!

If I found a treasure in my backyard while digging in the garden, I would…

If the President of the United States invited me to dinner, I would ask him if he would…

My favorite baseball player asked me to sit with him in the dugout for the big game.

Name _____ Date _____

Story Starter

If I had magical powers...

If I were marooned on an uninhabited island...

If I could read peoples' minds...

While I was watching television last night, the screen went blank during the commercials and the television talked to me.

Name _____ Date _____

Story Starter

The sport that my friends and I like to watch on television is _____ because...

Whenever I look through a newspaper the first thing I like to read is _____ because...

My _____ (brother/sister/cousin) can be irritating at times but I appreciate _____ (him/her) most when...

I like to walk in the woods on a beautiful fall day because...

Name _____ Date _____

Story Starter

My favorite season of the year is _____ because...

I love celebrating the Fourth of July because...

The most fascinating thing to me about the history of my town/city is...

Stories about _____ are interesting to me because...

0-7424-1785-9 *After School Writing Activities*

Name _____ Date _____

Story Starter

If I could visit any country in the world, I would visit _____ because...

My family is very special because...

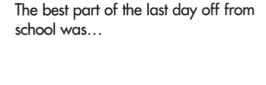

The best part of the last day off from school was...

It's wonderful being friends with _____ because...

0-7424-1785-9 *After School Writing Activities*

Name _____ Date _____

Story Starter

If I were ten years older, I would...

For Halloween, I'd like to go as my hero, _____ , because...

The thing that I love best about Christmas is...

If I could go on a cruise, I'd like to go to _____ because...

What is Poetry?

Our first experience with poetry is usually nursery rhymes. But there's a whole lot more besides nursery rhymes. A poem tells about feelings, ideas, events, or they can be imaginative exercises. Most poetry has a musical quality. A sense of **rhythm** is accomplished by choosing words that not only mean what you want to say, but sound good when you say them together.

For example, imagine that you want to write a poem that tells how much you like homework. You might say "I like homework." It says what you mean, but doesn't really sound poetic, does it? So you might want to try something like "My homework happiness knows no bounds." Repeating these sounds makes the sentence more musical and poetic.

h sound with **h**omework and **h**appiness
m sound with **M**y and ho**m**ework
n sound with k**n**ows, **n**o, and bou**n**ds
s sound with happine**ss**, know**s**, and bound**s**

Repeating letter sounds is called **alliteration**. Alliteration is one of many **poetic devices** that poets use as tools to make their poems more musical.

Identify the alliteration in the following sentences. What letters does the poet use for alliteration? Hint: Some sentences have more than one use of alliteration.

1. Tiger, tiger, burning bright in the forests of the night.—*William Blake*

2. My love is like a red, red rose.—*Robert Burns*

3. To be or not to be, that is the question.—*William Shakespeare*

4. When April with his showers sweet with fruit/The drought of March has pierced unto the root.—*Geoffrey Chaucer*

Name _____ Date _____

What Is Poetry? (continued from page 108)

You've probably noticed that a lot of poetry seems complicated. A confused reader might ask, "Why don't those poets just say what they mean?" The answer is that they are saying what they mean, but they're using language that describes not only what they mean but also how they feel toward what they're writing about.

For example, when T.S. Eliot started his famous poem *The Wasteland* with the line, "April is the cruelest month," he could have written, "I don't like April. To some, it may mean springtime, but it just makes me sad." The two lines say the same thing, but they mean two entirely different things. Eliot was using poetic devices to express a powerful feeling in a new, exciting, and different way.

The nineteenth century English poet, William Wordsworth defined poetry as "powerful emotion recollected in tranquility." Here's one example of how a poet quietly recalls a powerful emotion.

Once upon a midnight dreary, while I pondered, weak and weary,
Over many a quaint and curious volume of forgotten lore—
While I nodded, nearly napping, suddenly there came a tapping,
As of some one gently rapping, rapping at my chamber door.
"'Tis some visitor", I muttered, "tapping at my chamber door—
Only this and nothing more."

—Edgar Allen Poe

Without reading the rest of the poem, write how you think Poe continued with his poem.
Hint: The poem's title is The Raven.

Go to the library with a friend and take out a book of Edgar Allen Poe's poems that has *The Raven* in it. When you get home, take turns reading it aloud to *hear* how effective and powerful this poem is. Write a poem about an experience you've had that really affected you.

The Fearless and Fugitive Fido

A lot of poems begin with an *image* to express a powerful emotion. An image is a description that makes you feel something. Let's say that Fido, your pet boa constrictor ran away. But writing "My pet ran away" doesn't tell a reader anything about how you feel about your poor, lost Fido. A good image that shows you feel sad is:

> The glass cage is empty.

Now your reader has a mental picture of a glass cage, and they know it's empty but they don't know why. So you've given them a feeling, or *emotion*, to make them interested in the rest of your poem.

You could follow that image with another image or use another poetic device. Remember that a poetic device is a word or group of words that are used creatively to create the *sound, rhythm,* and *meaning* of your poem. There are many to choose from, but let's use alliteration:

> The silent slithering of my sneaky snake,
> the fearless and fugitive Fido.

Now your readers know that Fido is a snake who is probably still alive, quietly hiding somewhere. Now it is up to the poet to give the poem meaning:

I'll find him in the backyard alive and well chasing frogs.

Ask a friend to help you think of an occasion when you experienced something together that greatly influenced you both. Work together to write a four-line poem about it.

Name _____ Date _____

Show, Don't Tell

The golden rule of all good poetry writing is "Show, don't tell." Showing makes your reader *see*, *smell*, *feel*, *taste*, or *hear* what you are writing about. Telling is a quick way to let your reader know what you think, but showing tells them what you *feel*.

Let's go back to the poem that was begun on page 108. The telling version begins with:

        I like homework.

The showing version begins with:

        My homework happiness knows no bounds.

The showing version replaces *like* with *happiness*. This shows your reader more fully how you feel about homework. *Knows no bounds* shows the reader that the happiness you feel is complete. Write three more lines to go with the line above using imagery.

The English poet William Wordsworth wrote:

        My heart leaps up when I behold
        a rainbow in the sky.

1. Is Wordsworth showing or telling? Explain your answer.

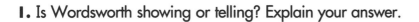

_____

_____

2. Which of the following is Wordsworth feeling?
    a. sadness   **b.** joy
    c. anger   **d.** stress

Wordsworth is stumped. Finish his poem for him. Remember to show how you feel by creating images. Read your poems to each other.

Name _____ Date _____

News that Stays News

The poet and critic Ezra Pound wrote that poetry is "news that stays news." By this he meant that a poem should mean as much today as it did yesterday or tomorrow. A poem that expresses a feeling accurately will always be news to new generations of readers. That is why poets such as William Shakespeare—who died in 1616—are still very popular today. One of Shakespeare's most famous poems begins:

>   Shall I compare thee to a summer's day?
>   Thou art more lovely and more temperate.

Confused? Don't be! Shakespeare was writing a long time ago when people actually talked this way. But what he was writing about and the way he expressed it is still news today.

1. What is Shakespeare asking in the poem's first line?
    a. If he can go on a picnic.
    b. If summer vacation will start soon.
    c. If he can compare summer and winter.
    d. If he can compare a person to a summer's day.

2. Who or what is "more lovely and more temperate?"
    a. A summer's day
    b. The poet's girlfriend or boyfriend
    c. Shakespeare
    d. Art

Write a four-line poem using poetic imagery to show how you feel about someone who is special to you.

Read other poems by William Shakespeare. You and a friend can find them on the Internet or at the library. Even though his poems were written long ago, try to figure out together the meaning or what his poems are describing.

0-7424-1785-9 *After School Writing Activities*

Name _____ Date _____

Couplets and Quatrains

A **couplet** is two lines that rhyme. A **quatrain** is two couplets, which is four lines. The poetic lines below are marked **a** or **b**. The **a** lines rhyme with the other **a** lines, and **b** lines rhyme with **b** lines. This is known as a **rhyme scheme**. Normally the lines are the same length and combine to complete a thought.

Sometimes the rhymes are apart like this:

My mother gets so mad when I don't clean my room,	**a**
She gives me all kinds of strife.	**b**
She opens my door and throws in a broom,	**a**
And threatens to ground me for life!	**b**

A poem may also follow an **abba** and **aabb** rhyme scheme.

April is my favorite month because I get to play in the mud.
It splatters my clothes, making them wet.

Finish the quatrain using the lines below. Keep in mind all the rhyme scheme possibilities!

1. A good third line would read:
   a. I make mud pies that my sister eats.
   b. I have to wash off when I get home.
   c. Do I enjoy myself? You bet!
   d. My dog gets dirtier than me.

2. A good fourth line would read:
   a. Until my boots start to flood.
   b. I fall into a puddle.
   c. My mother is mad at me.
   d. It begins to rain again.

Finish the following couplet. Remember to rhyme! Have a friend finish it too and see how many possibilities there are.

The mountain stands majestic and tall

0-7424-1785-9 *After School Writing Activities*

Five-Line Fun

A **limerick** is a five-line poem with an **aabba** rhyme scheme. Because limericks are usually funny, they are some of the most fun poems to read or write. Writing limericks is also good practice for rhyming and **rhythm**. Rhythm is perhaps the most important poetic device, because rhythm determines the overall sound of a poem.

The rhythm of a limerick is simply achieved by counting the syllables in each line. Lines one, two, and five rhyme and usually contain eight to ten syllables. Lines three and four have a different rhyme and only contain five to seven syllables. An example of a limerick and the number of syllables appears below:

There was a food critic from Howell	**a 9 syllables**
Who scrunched up his face in a scowl	**a 9 syllables**
While out dining on pheasant	**b 7 syllables**
In the town of Mt. Pleasant	**b 7 syllables**
He declared it murder most fowl.	**b 9 syllables**

Notice how the poet added a syllable to the words "scowl" and "fowl" to make it rhyme with the two-syllable word "Howell."

Now it's your turn to finish a limerick. Make sure you count the syllables and follow the **aabba** rhyme scheme!

_____

Who lived in a house by the sea

_____

and swallowed it whole

_____

Have a limerick competition. See who can write the most, the funniest, and the cleverest limericks. Don't be afraid to be silly! Have a teacher, friend, or family member be the judge.

Name _____ Date _____

Japanese Poetic Forms

Haiku and **tanka** are two poetic forms that come from Japan. Both follow a strict number of syllables in each line of the poem. The subjects of haiku and tankas usually have to do with some aspect of nature and contain only a single thought about a special moment.

Haiku
A three-line poem of 17 syllables
Line 1: 5 syllables
Line 2: 7 syllables
Line 3: 5 syllables

Haiku
It is late summer   **5 syllables**
The golden rod and ragweed **7 syllables**
Pollinate my nose   **5 syllables**

A bear chased my dad   **5 syllables**
All the way home from hunting **7 syllables**
Next year he will fish   **5 syllables**

Tanka
A five-line poem of 31 syllables
Line 1: 5 syllables
Line 2: 7 syllables
Line 3: 5 syllables
Line 4: 7 syllables
Line 5: 7 syllables

Tanka
How could I be anything   **7 syllables**
but a mountain goat **5 syllables**
on a day like this —   **5 syllables**
brilliant blue sky, white clouds   **7 syllables**
and the earth sheltered with snow! **7 syllables**

To write your own haiku or tanka, go outside and sit for a few minutes. Ask a friend to join you. Notice the sights and sounds around you. Write your thoughts down as a poem. Choose words that will help your reader feel as though he or she had been sitting beside you as you wrote.

Name _____ Date _____

My Love Is Like...

One poetic device that poets use to compare is a **simile**. Remember that a simile usually includes the words *like* or *as*.

For example, the Scottish poet Robert Burns wrote: "My love is like a red, red rose." By saying *like* a red, red rose, Burns isn't saying that his love is a rose, but that she has certain qualities that remind him of a rose. This is the picture that he wants his reader to see.

Another example of a simile is from William Wordsworth, who wrote "I wandered lonely as a cloud."

Of course, Wordsworth wasn't a cloud but he creates an interesting image, doesn't he? Is a cloud lonely? Well, it might be if it had feelings. But Wordsworth was creating an image of a single cloud drifting through an empty sky.

You're the poet. You want to use a simile that talks about how much you like your new socks. Which of the following examples would you use?

  a. My new socks are red and really cool.
  b. I admire my socks as a dog views a bone.
  c. I am humble in the presence of my socks.
  d. There's a pair of socks that I like very much.

Look at the objects in the room where you are sitting. Compare these objects to people you know. Make a list of similes. For example: My little brother is like a book. Show your similes to your friend and have him or her complete the comparisons.

Name _____ Date _____

Love is a Rose

Using metaphors in poetry helps to create the image that you want your reader to see. A **metaphor** states that one kind of object or idea is something that it really isn't.

The poet John Ciardi wrote the metaphor, "The paper fields lay crumpled by the road." His metaphor compares the fields to paper, even though we know that fields are not made of paper. He adds the image "lay crumpled by the road" to help his metaphor make more sense.

Robert Burns wrote the simile, "His love is like a rose." The songwriter Neil Young wrote the metaphor "Love is a rose." He has created an image of something beautiful yet delicate. The rest of the line reads "But you better not pick it. It only grows when it's on the vine." A nice image!

1. Complete the following metaphors.

    a. My heart is stone _____.

    b. My soul is an eagle _____.

    c. The classroom is a zoo _____.

    d. The dinner table was a battlefield _____.

2. Find the metaphor.

    a. Quiet as a church mouse

    b. Fists like Virginia hams

    c. Just like Romeo and Juliet

    d. The rosy-fingered dawn

With a friend, write down a list of descriptions of each of your bedrooms at home. Discuss how they look using metaphors and write them down. For example: My bedroom was hit by a tornado. Trade your descriptions and discuss them.

poetry skills   Name _____ Date _____

Knows No Bounds!

Read the following poem and answer the questions.

My homework happiness knows no bounds!
I devour every book I take home.
I'm like a pack of wild and hungry hounds
When it's off to the library I roam.

1. The poem above is an example of
   a. a limerick
   b. a quatrain
   c. a tanka
   d. a haiku

2. The third line is an example of
   a. a tanka
   b. a metaphor
   c. a limerick
   d. a simile

3. The rhyme scheme is
   a. aabb
   b. abab
   c. abba
   d. baba

Write a quatrain using one of the rhyme schemes about something that makes you happy.

Write a four-line poem like the one above with a friend. Each of you write two lines that rhyme.

0-7424-1785-9 After School Writing Activities

Name _____ Date _____

Merrily We Roll Along

One of the reasons songs are enjoyed by so many people is because their words, called **lyrics**, speak to the listener.

Songs are usually written in verses with a **chorus**, which is repeated throughout the song. Most songs use **end rhyme**, which means the words at the end of the lines of the song rhyme. Like poems and stories, songs have **themes**. This is the message the songwriter is trying to convey to the listener through the song.

Listen to one of your favorite songs while you are looking at the lyrics. Then answer the following questions.

1. What is the song mostly about?

_____

2. How does the song make you feel?_____

3. What do you think is the theme of the song?_____

4. How many verses does the song have?_____

5. Does the song use end rhyme?_____ If so, give an example

from the song: _____

_____

6. Does the song have a chorus?_____

7. What is it about this song that makes it one of your favorites? _____

_____

Use a tune from a song and collaborate with a friend to write lyrics to go with the music. Be sure to keep your lyrics in the right rhythm with the music. Share your song with friends and family.

Name _____ Date _____

Please Elaborate

Once you've written a first draft, go back and **revise** to make your writing more clear. One way to do this is to **elaborate** by adding details. Using *examples*, *explanations*, and *descriptions* help add more detail.

before revising: Unusual colors glowed in the sky.
after revising: Streaks of green, blue, and red glowed in the sky.

Read each sentence. The hint tells what kind of detail would make the sentence better. Circle the letter of the revised sentence that adds that type of detail.

1. The aurora borealis are beautiful. (*add description*)
  a. The aurora borealis are dazzling ray-filled curtains of red, blue, and green.
  b. The aurora borealis are a result of charged particles from the sun.
  c. The aurora borealis are often seen in Canada, Alaska, and Greenland.

2. The aurora borealis are made up of glowing particles. (*explain*)
  a. The aurora borealis are bands of red, blue, and green light from the air.
  b. The aurora borealis are a result of charged particles from the sun hitting our air.
  c. The aurora borealis are most often seen in the upper atmosphere.

3. The colors come from different air molecules. (*give examples*)
  a. The colors are dazzling reds, blues, and greens from air molecules.
  b. The different colors come from air molecules like oxygen, which produces yellow-green.
  c. Nitrogen makes one of the colors of the aurora.

Read the sentence. Then, revise it to add the type of detail given in the hint.
4. The aurora borealis are colorful. (*add description*)

_____

Write a story about the worst storm you can remember experiencing. Have your friend do the same. Exchange stories and elaborate by adding details to each other's sentences.

Name _____ Date _____

Using Commas Correctly

Commas are used to signal pauses or slight distinctions between words in sentences. When you are proofreading your writing, check to make sure that you have used commas properly. They should:

✔ separate each item in a list of three or more items
✔ separate two or more adjectives in place of *and*
✔ set off the words *yes* and *no* or the name of the person you are talking to
✔ separate the day from the year in a date
✔ separate the street, city, and state or country in an address

Examples: I had a sandwich, a glass of milk, and a cookie for lunch.
It was a clean, tidy kitchen.
Yes, I'm hungry. Marcus, are you hungry?
She was born on May 23, 1990.
I live at 1046 Mapleview Ave., Bangor, Maine.

Put in commas where they are needed in the following sentences.

1. Camille pushed open the old creaky door.

2. The only things in the room were a desk a chair and a candle.

3. Rudolf are you ready to go? Yes I'm ready to go.

4. They were sent to 47 West 10th St. Abilene Texas to discover the missing clue.

5. The ghost was first seen in the house on December 24 1894.

 Make up a story with a friend using the sentences you corrected. After writing it, have your friend proofread it.

Name _____ Date _____

Writing Quotations Correctly

Quotation marks show exactly what the speaker said. A conversation in a story is written as a dialogue. When using dialogue, every speaker begins in a new paragraph to make it easier to keep track of different speakers. The first word in a quotation is capitalized. The words within a quotation can end in a comma, question mark, or exclamation point. They never end in a period unless it marks the end of a sentence. See the example below.

"Did you go to the Halloween party last night?" asked Kristine.

"Yes, Kristine, I came as a pirate," replied Tuan.

Kristine said, "Who else was there?"

"Just about everyone in our class. It was so much fun. We laughed so hard when Fritz got his head stuck in a pumpkin."

Add the missing punctuation in the quotations below.

1. Where were you at 2:30 on the morning of the fifteenth asked the lawyer.

2. I was in the kitchen replied the witness.

3. And what were you doing in the kitchen he exclaimed.

4. I was making a… a… turkey sandwich he stammered.

5. Exactly what did you put in your turkey sandwich Mr. Boise asked the lawyer, with a triumphant gleam in his eye.

6. The witness licked his lips nervously and whispered Lettuce, tomato, mayonnaise and bacon.

Write a conversation you've had recently with a friend. Use the correct punctuation marks to show a direct quotation. Ask your friend to do the same and check each other's quotations.

Name _____ Date _____

Making Subjects and Verbs Agree

Every sentence has a subject and a verb. Present-tense verbs have two forms: the **plain form,** like *walk,* and the **s form,** like *walks.* The verb form must agree with the subject.

When the subject is a singular noun or the pronoun, *it, she,* or *he,* use the **s form** of the verb.

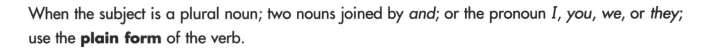

Example: Elsa **walks** to school every day.

When the subject is a plural noun; two nouns joined by *and;* or the pronoun *I, you, we,* or *they;* use the **plain form** of the verb.

Example: Elsa and Xenia **walk** to school every day.

Underline the correct form of the present-tense verb in the following sentences.

1. Every day I (jog, jogs) in the park.
2. My brother (run, runs) three miles before school.
3. He (go, goes) around the park four times.
4. My two golden retrievers usually (scurry, scurries) next to me as I jog.
5. Sometimes they (take, takes) off after a squirrel.
6. Two police officers always (pass, passes) us in the park.
7. They (smile, smiles) and (wave, waves) at us.

Write a short diary entry for your favorite TV or book character, telling what you think she or he might be doing now. Use present-tense verb forms. Underline each verb form you use.

Write a story about what you did with a friend last Saturday. Have your friend write a story about the same experience. Trade stories and check to make sure the verb form agrees with the subject. Combine your stories into one story.

Name _____ Date _____

Do You Hafe a Brother?

When you proofread your writing or another person's writing, you check to find errors. Check the advertisements below for **spelling errors,** and make sure that the **verb form and subjects agree**. Cross out the misspelled words and write the corrected words above them.

Gum-Everlasting

Does your gum lose its flavor?

Dose it gets hard after only twelve hours?

You need too try new Gum-Everlasting.

WHY?

Yule get all-day chewing enjoyment!

You'll also get our new, high-tech Gum Reflaviator. Put you're old gum inside the Reflaviator befor you go to bed. When you get up in the morning, your gum is sotf, flavorful, and ready for another day. So, bye your Gum-Everlasting today!

Brother Be-Gone

Rose had a big problem—her brothers. When she goed to her room to play with her friends, her brothers allways followed them. Thay teased Rose and laught at her.

Rose tryed Brother Be-Gone. She sprayed Brother Be-Gon around her room. That was the end of her problem! Roses brotters stood by the door, but they could'nt came into her room.

Do you hafe a brother? You need Brother Be-Gone!

Work with a friend to think of two brand-new toys. Write advertisements for the toys. Proofread each other's advertisements for spelling, punctuation, capitalization, and complete sentences.

0-7424-1785-9 *After School Writing Activities*

Name _____ Date _____

Proofreading Fun

Symbol	Meaning
∧	Insert a letter, word, phrase, or sentence.
ℐ	Take out a letter, word, phrase, or sentence.
⊙	Insert a period.
/	Change a capital letter to a small letter.
≡	Change a small letter to a capital letter.
(SP)	Check the spelling of a word.

Use these proofreading symbols to help you understand what corrections need to be made in these sentences. Write the sentences correctly on a separate sheet of paper.

1. Everyone knows ∧ᵗʰᵉ best way to keeep fish from ℐmelling is to cut off their noses.

2. a̲ fence runs all around the the ℐard, but never moves⊙

3. t̲he rug told ∧ᵗʰᵉ floor, "don't move, I've got you covered.̲"

4. The ℐelephone rang just as I stepped in the door. I quickly answered it⊙ What a nice surprise ∧ⁱᵗ was to hear from Uncle j̲oe in Providence, r̲hode Island. He asked if I would like to fly out to visit him this summer. I asked my Mom and Dad, and they said I could go. I can't wait. What a thrilling ℐummer it will bee!
(SP)

Write five sentences with two mistakes in each sentence. Have a friend do the same. Trade papers and proofread each other's work.

0-7424-1785-9 *After School Writing Activities*

Answer Key

Nature's Grand Light Show **6**
    1. c; **2.** a; **3.** b

Picture It! **7**
    1. tell; **2.** show; **5.** 4

The Street Is Alive **9**
    1. bustles, give way, crowd, breathes, are dressed, beckon, is alive,
    2. threatens, sustained, wear, are, attending, swing, swirl and waltz, blows in, sings,

Like a Bowl Full of Jelly **10**
    5 similes—cheeks were like roses; nose like a cherry; the beard on his chin was as white as the snow; smoke it encircled his head like a wreath; shook when he laughed like a bowl full of jelly

As Gentle as a Lamb **11**
    1. swan; **2.** drums; **3.** fish; **4.** rock

You're a Dream Come True **12**
    1. c; **2.** c; **3.** c; **4.** b

As Sweet as Pie **13**
    1. M; **2.** S; **3.** S; **4.** M; **5.** S; **6.** M; **7.** S; **8.** M

I Could Sleep for a Year! **14**
    1. H; **2.** H; **4.** H; **6.** H; **7.** H

Whirl! **15**
    1. whirled; **2.** snap; **3.** rattled; **4.** ribbit, chirping, croak, caws, whistles, trills, buzz

Answer, Respond, Reply Crossword **16**

Across

1. wish	**28.** cast
4. stamp	**30.** lies
7. slant	**32.** totes
9. lend	**36.** catch
12. talked	**37.** burst
14. lift	**38.** err
15. lock	**39.** pull
16. arouse	**40.** rot
19. apes	**41.** adore
20. laid	**42.** alarm
21. aged	**43.** ensnared
24. gleamed	**44.** skim
27. run	**45.** use

Down

1. walks	**22.** get
2. ink	**23.** bust
3. steal	**25.** ate
5. toiled	**26.** pat
6. meet	**27.** rests
7. stop	**28.** call
8. laced	**29.** scares
10. elude	**30.** lure
11. dream	**31.** irons
13. drag	**32.** tear
15. land	**33.** order
17. oil	**34.** trod
18. froth	**35.** speak
	36. claim

Lost and Found Crossword **17**

Across

2. less	**26.** he
5. moist	**28.** son
8. slow	**31.** men
11. above	**33.** out
13. on	**35.** right
16. evening	**39.** obey
17. laughs	**41.** own
20. no	**43.** doer
21. lent	**44.** swim
22. guess	**45.** die
23. good	**46.** mild
24. stop	**47.** wet
25. her	**48.** straight

Down

1. ma	**24.** snub
2. loved	**26.** hot
3. even	**29.** now
4. sent	**30.** them
5. mighty	**31.** my
6. ill	**32.** new
7. tough	**34.** under
9. lass	**36.** idle
10. won	**37.** go
12. below	**38.** trim
14. none	**39.** old
15. bigger	**40.** east
18. guest	**42.** went
19. hero	**44.** sea

Good Grief! **18**
    1. calm wind
    2. cowardly lion
    3. old news
    4. pretty ugly

Combining Words **19**

2. eye + brow = eyebrow	**9.** lady + bug = ladybug
3. port + able = portable	**10.** pig + tail = pigtail
4. be + long = belong	**11.** rebel + lion = rebellion
5. pal + ace = palace	**12.** hand + shake = handshake
6. hum + or = humor	**13.** ad + age = adage
7. car + ton = carton	**14.** mush + room = mushroom
8. bed + room = bedroom	**15.** per + form = perform

Fun with Word Endings **20**
    1. actor
    2. politely
    3. tricky
    4. freedom
    5. friendly, friendship, friendliness, friendless

0-7424-1785-9 *After School Writing Activities*